The Essentials of Cabin Living, What You Need to Know

By Russ Steffy

ISBN-13:9781494203153

About This Guide

The Essentials of Cabin Living is a blend of true stories of the author's personal experiences relevant to rural cabin living and a guide designed for those who wish to live rurally but seek direction from other rural dwellers as to what to expect and how to prepare for a significant change in lifestyle. Transitioning to a cabin setting, whether in the mountains, plains, or desert can pay tremendous dividends by offering a stress free environment in a natural setting replete of indigenous wildlife. However, all dividends are accompanied by a price. The objective of *The Essentials of Cabin Living* is to lower that price as much as possible, if not eliminate it altogether. The location of the cabin, surrounding terrain, magnitude of the impact of each season, and the amenities of the cabin itself will determine how much and what type of maintenance of the structure and surrounding area may require, equipment necessary for maintenance, what provisions must be stored, and bug out plans in the event of an emergency.

Rural living means that most cabin dwellers are considerably farther from first responders such as law enforcement, fire, and paramedic services than those who live in urban areas. Emergency preparedness is a vital practice which should be constantly addressed by everyone; however rural residents can be on their own for extended periods of time and therefore must be better prepared for any situation which may arise. *The Essentials of Cabin Living* covers dozens of scenarios from life threatening wildfires to frozen water pipes along with a host of recommendations for these and other events. *The Essentials of Cabin Living* includes comprehensive lists of suggested equipment, provisions, and strategies for living safely and comfortably in a rural setting.

Acknowledgments

The Essentials of Cabin Living is dedicated to all First Responders whether they may be Fire Fighters, Law Enforcement Officers, or Paramedics. What I owe them I will never be able to repay in full. But I do my best to reciprocate by abiding by, and when necessary, enforce the laws, both written and unwritten, to protect a lifestyle of which so many are so passionate.

I also wish to offer a very special "Thank You" to the Red Cross and the County Engineers.

"It was the best of times, it was the worst of times..."
Charles Dickens

About the Author

I am an avid outdoorsman and in addition to possessing over forty years of camping and backpacking experience in a variety of environments, I am privileged to have spent nearly twenty years in a 1200 square foot rural cabin high up in the coastal mountains of California. But let me be clear about what I am not; I do not claim to be a survivalist, doomsday prepper, or licensed contractor. I am not qualified to offer recommendations with regards to any aspect of building or renovating structures for the purpose of use as living quarters. I have little experience living in a snowbound cabin setting for any significant length of time and I make no recommendations for rural living in snowbound environments.

The Essentials of Cabin Living is my autobiography of sorts detailing the challenges and rewards of rural living. Everything I learned and have offered in this guide about rural living is the result of trial and error as I was alone among family and friends for any reliance or guidance for a lifestyle of which they knew even less than I. Because of my camping and backpacking experience, most of my errors sided on trivial matters rather than life threatening situations.

Common sense, planning ahead, and preparation are essential for achieving comfort, safety, and simplicity. Just like our urban counterparts, emergency plans should be designed and practiced, extra provisions should be stock piled, and portable stoves and lanterns along with fuel should be maintained and stored for either hunkering down or bugging out. No detail should be overlooked, for example, parking your vehicle heading away from your cabin can save you precious seconds should a wildfire approach unexpectedly.

There is risk versus reward in every aspect of one's life and I have introduced you to a brief summary of perhaps the risk of what cabin living may entail. The rewards of rural living outweigh risk logarithmically so long as the risk has been mitigated. Daily hikes into the surroundings in pure solitude and clean air, and where your closest neighbor is a half mile away or more, sitting outside on quiet evenings without the noise from the nearest road, and knowing getting up the next morning can be more of the same if you desire. This is what I have been so fortunate to experience.

Table of Contents

CHAPTER 5 PREPARATION, PREVENTION AND PROPERTY MAINTENANCE 60

CHAPTER 6 EMERGENCY PREPAREDNESS..........68

Chapter 1 The Beginning, and the First Challenge

After ending a tumultuous first marriage I found a small cabin situated high up in the coastal mountains of California. I wanted to be far enough away from my ex-wife yet still be geographically close to family and friends. My commute time to the office increased considerably, but I was fortunate enough such that I could telecommute about half the time. The cabin is located in a rural area with my closest neighbor about a half mile away and the only paved road another half mile beyond. My cabin is just a few minutes walk from a back entrance to a Federal Conservancy, basically hundreds of square miles of parkland set aside from development and jointly managed by the U.S. Park Service, the State Parks, and the surrounding counties. This location offers instant access to all the hiking and mountain biking one could ever want. When everything is working, my cabin has running water, electricity, septic, and a fifty gallon propane tank which has to be filled about once a month. Only the kitchen stove and hot water heater are hooked up to the propane tank as drying clothes using either a gas or electric dryer is just too expensive. Heat for the cabin is provided exclusively by a wood burning stove. One of the prerequisites for living in my new home was to re-learn all of the methods for splitting logs and cutting them to size. The old saying "firewood warms you twice" couldn't have been more appropriate. The little wood burning stove did a wonderful job. Just so you have some an idea how cold it does get, every year the pipes freeze several times. In fact, the lowest temperature my thermometer reading ever showed was 18 degrees (F).

The cabin was small, maybe twelve hundred square feet with two bedrooms, a small kitchen and bath, and the living room as the center of the structure. The original four walls of the cabin were built back in the early 1920's by a well known politician of the time. As a young man, he built the cabin to serve as a hunting lodge. Over the years people who had lived in the cabin added "improvements", all of which were amateur at best. Constant maintenance was required to keep the roof from leaking, keeping the critters out, replacing leaking pipes, and cleaning the wood burning stove vent. If you have ever lived more than a week in an isolated cabin, you know how much work is involved just sweeping up the dust and dirt that quickly accumulates inside. These issues became minor inconveniences over time as I adjusted to isolated living. The real pay off was living in a lush, virtually untouched wilderness area complete with coyotes, bobcats, raccoons, and yes, snakes and other creepy crawlies! Looking closely at this side view approaching the cabin, you can barely make out the cabin as it was painted to blend in with the surroundings:

Several years passed after I moved to my cabin when I met my future wife whom I dated for several more years. Nothing much in way of excitement occurred during that time, and I was just as happy for that. My new wife ultimately moved in with me, however the successive years of peace and tranquility were about to present challenges of which I could have never imagined (not because of my new wife, though!).

The month after my wife moved into our little cabin saw one of the largest wildfires in California history sweep through tens of thousands of acres all the way to the coastline where scores of beachfront mansions were burned to the ground. I had driven into the city for errands and found out about the wildfire around 10:30am, I believe on a weekday. Reports were broadcast that the fire was closing in on the area where our cabin was. I immediately went back home as my wife was there alone and without a vehicle. In hindsight, of course, that wasn't a brilliant idea on my part and have long since remedied that situation.

The drive home was like something out of a disaster movie. The highway up the coast was the only way to get to our cabin from the south side of the coastal mountains. It is a four lane highway with two lanes for each direction, but a lot of folks were hurrying home as I was. Everyone could see dark brown smoke rising thousands of feet in the air, and everyone knew this thing was getting real close. Panic set in, people were driving north in southbound lanes, driving on the right shoulder, and otherwise driving at excessive speeds while making dangerous maneuvers through traffic. I drove a truck at the time so I had no choice but to be patient. I certainly felt a sense of urgency, though getting myself killed in a traffic collision wasn't going to help matters.

The Village, as the locals called it, is a small shopping area with a general store, a few small businesses, a boutique, and the Post Office. The Village is located several miles from our cabin. The Village served as a central location for the locals to gather not unlike any other small community. I arrived at the Village just before authorities' shutdown both local roads into and out of the area. In particular, they closed the road from the Village leading the rest of the way to our cabin, and so I was faced with the task of somehow locating my wife. Thankfully my wife, along with several of our neighbors, had walked down the closed road from where our cabin was leading as many horses as each person could handle. I didn't know at the time, but it turns out my wife is quite knowledgeable about horses, and the neighbors praised her for her assistance. Unfortunately, she escaped with only what she was wearing at the time and what ever was in her hand bag.

The fire had already burned one home at the very top of the canyon, just a mile or so from our cabin. My wife and I along with dozens of fellow cabin dwellers spent the rest of the day milling about the Village waiting for anything newsworthy. Evening fell and there was no change in status. My wife and I finally headed away from The Village towards the valley side of the coastal mountains to get a room for the night. On the drive out of the canyon, which was the opposite direction of the path of the fire, we pulled over at one of the vistas and looked in awe as we could see flames all over our beloved canyon shooting hundreds of feet in the air. All I could say was "well, this is going to be the easiest move I've ever had to do!"

We ended up staying a week in our motel room and even got a break in price because we had been displaced by the fire. After nearly a week, the fire was officially declared out and we were allowed to go home. I think I had the world's largest butterfly in my stomach as we pulled around the last bend to get our first look at what I figured would be nothing but ash. But to my amazement, our little cabin was completely untouched and intact in the middle of a field of ash. It turns out the Fire Fighters had used our cabin and surrounding land as a staging area for fire crews from all over California and even surrounding states. It was a strategic location because of the local topography. Keeping the fire from spreading from up and over the next canyon was the key to their success in saving all of the cabins in the immediate area. Residents raised their American flags and displayed signs of gratitude to the firefighters in front of their cabins and on their vehicles. Indeed, a remarkable feat.

The first night back was unnerving. There were still dozens of hot spots where smoke could be seen rising into the air. Perhaps a bit on the excessive compulsive side, I actually placed several smoke detectors around the outside of our cabin. None of them sounded and I don't know if my idea would have been any more than a false sense of security. Our cabin is situated on about twenty acres of hillside land all of which had been reduced to ash. We did our best to fill buckets with water and try to put them out, but I finally gave in to resisting calling the fire department. When the engine arrived I apologized to them repeatedly, but they just told me to relax and that I did the right thing. After all, nobody wanted to go through that nightmare again.

Chapter 2 The Aftermath, Not Out of the Woods Yet

Having just returned from a week away from our cabin, my wife and I awoke the next morning to knocks on our front door. I couldn't recall the last time a stranger knocked on the front door of our cabin in at least the past seven or eight years. I opened the door and there stood about a dozen folks from the Red Cross! They brought sandwiches, drinks, and believe it or not, shovels, sandbags, and a dump truck full of sand! I was speechless, but I welcomed the sight as it was comforting to know I had help I knew I was going to need but certainly didn't expect it to turn out like this. I spent several hours working alongside the Red Cross folks laying out sand bags in precise locations in anticipation of the flooding and mud slides that were sure to follow. It was November and the rainy season was just around the corner. I knew they couldn't spend all day with me as I knew my neighbors could use a hand as well, so I let them know I could finish up what we had started and thanked them for all they had done.

No sooner had the Red Cross folks left, a couple of engineers from the county showed up to help as well. I walked with the engineers around most of the perimeter of the twenty acres of hillside land I was situated on. They were concerned about water runoff, mudslides, and loose boulders tumbling into our cabin upon the next sizeable rainstorm. They had pre-printed topographic maps of the area on which they hand drew the recommended locations for sandbagging, trenching, and barriers.

I thanked them profusely for their help as they handed me the sketches I would need to follow all of their recommendations. After just this one day, I recaptured a lot of faith in the human race which I had lost over the past twenty years. But that's another story.

Out of the dozens of huge California Live Oak trees, only two were lost on the twenty acres of land surrounding our little cabin. Virtually all of the shrubbery, vines, brush, and grass had all turned to ash, only the hardiest of plant life survived. The hillside once covered with lush flora was now mostly a moonscape. You can see from this picture taken only a few weeks after the wildfire was completely put out the ground cover was already beginning to grow back:

With nothing to hold the topsoil in place during even a mild rainstorm, I had to start work on deploying the county engineer's recommendations immediately. The highest priority was completing the sandbagging. There were two normally dry creeks, one on either side of the cabin that would naturally control the runoff from the hillside behind. I had to stack enough sandbags to account for overflow because of the lack of vegetation which otherwise acts as resistance to the flow of water. The end result was about fifteen hundred sandbags creating walls two to three feet high and about two feet thick. The strategy for using sandbags is simple: they are not supposed to stop water or mudflow; rather they are used to redirect water and mudflow around the area to be protected.

My next priority was to construct several barriers. The type of barriers were nothing more than setting four by four posts into postholes five or six feet apart and secured with ready mix concrete. Nailing a thick sheet of plywood to each post would complete the barrier. The trick was to construct the barrier in locations to protect, for example, the plate glass windows and the water heater from free falling boulders. The final tasks were clearing the natural drainage and the trenching all the way up to the top of the hillsides of anything which could allow the runoff to overflow and flood the cabin.

A lot of debris including almost cut to size logs had been left in the natural drainage by the fire crews. No complaints, that provided us with free fire wood for the entire following year! (It takes a year or more for wood to "season" or dry depending on the type). We also pulled at least a half dozen mattresses which might have been there for the twenty or thirty years. We never saw the old remains of the mattresses before the fire because there was too much vegetation hiding them from view.

Trenching amounted to literally digging small trenches along the contour of the exposed hillside but angled down slightly towards the natural drainage creeks. Any runoff would be directed to the natural drainage instead of creating uncontrolled new channels. My wife and I worked until sundown every day and managed to complete all of these preparations in about a month, and that was going to be "just in time".

The First Storm

With nothing to hold soil in place and slow the rainfall down, what was normally a small dry creek bed became a raging river. At the bend below our cabin, I had previously measured the height between the creek bottom and the road surface which was about 25 feet. The width between the canyon walls at road level was about 50 feet. At its highest point, the creek-turned-river overflowed the road but not quite enough to keep trucks from crossing. The water was an astonishing grey-black opaque color with a luster like the volcanic rock called obsidian. It was only beautiful in the sense it was a by product of an act of nature. The sky was ominously dark when the photograph below was taken within just an hour or so after the first heavy rain fell. Unfortunately, this picture is not as candid as if you were actually there:

The real ugliness came in the form of propane tanks, trash containers, lawn furniture, and children's toys of all sorts which washed down the creek with nothing to stop it. The water was so high and the current so swift, a mid-sized car was actually washed away and later found about fifteen feet up a tree. Fortunately, there were no human casualties.

This next photograph shows the creek a couple of days after the first heavy rainfall. The ash has already been swept away, now the unprotected top soil follows:

Flash Floods

As long as we are on the subject, and since I do a lot of
primitive camping, one of the acts of nature I am always on
the look out for is any potential for flash flooding. There is
a reason why flash floods are called what they are – the
flooding can occur before you realize what is actually
happening. For example, potential spots for construction of
out buildings must be evaluated in anticipation of any
possibility for floods. The cause is typically sudden heavy
rainfall in a short period of time. However, you must
realize it could be raining heavily dozens of miles up the
river or dry canyon where you may not be aware of the
potential for flooding. The rule is simple: always assume
the possibility of flash flooding and select a site for an out
building or equipment storage appropriately. A spot on or
towards the peak of a hill or knoll would be a much better
choice over a dry river bed.

Incidentally, localized flash flooding has also been known to be caused by the failure of a natural barrier upriver. The barrier could be a combination of boulders and fallen trees which have accumulated in one particular spot over many years resulting in a sort of natural dam. Even dens built by beavers have been known to burst, causing flooding downstream. We all know what happens when a dam gives way.

One experience I had was during a day picnic alongside a large creek. It was a warm, sunny day without a cloud in sight. I watched the kids playing along side the creek while sneaking a moment here and there to read. At one point I looked up from my book and noticed the creek had grown into a river and was about to make an island out our shoreline picnic spot! Within just a few of minutes, kids and picnic items were packed up and we proceeded to move to higher ground. After an hour or so the river receded back to being a creek and we resumed our picnic. I never did find out what happened that afternoon, but I'll never forget how quickly the landscape had changed.

Chapter 3 More to Come

At 4:30am the following January, we had a replay of a major earthquake which struck California back in 1971. Called the Northridge Quake, it was just as terrifying and just as devastating. My wife and I were asleep when it hit. My first thought was a propane truck had exploded next to our cabin. A few seconds later I realized we were experiencing a major earthquake. Most everything in Southern California driven by electricity went dark. I went outside to check the foundation of the cabin and generally just to make sure water and gas pipes were not broken. However, the damage was done, our septic system failed. Oh goody, I get to dig the thing up to find out where and what is broken. At least you know when you're getting close! Unfortunately, I dug up the entire system from the house to the tank without finding any problems. That could mean only one thing; the problem is on the other side of the tank. Sure enough, the earthquake had shifted the entire 1500 gallon septic tank about a foot snapping the piping from the tank to the leach line. I bought a couple of PVC elbows and kicked them into place, problem solved!

Just as I had finished repairing the septic system, the next of the heavy rains of the season came, and this was when I got my first lucky break since the fire last November. Only by pure luck and coincidence did I shovel all of the dirt from the trench I dug to expose the septic system onto the uphill side. The rainstorm lasting several days washed all the dirt back into the trench saving me hours of back breaking work! And, all of the sandbagging, trenching, and clearing of drainage paid off. Not a single drop of water entered the cabin.

Life in general gradually went back to peaceful serenity. Although the new moonscape took some getting used to, we knew everything would grow back in just a couple of years. Meanwhile, my wife tended her garden and turned some of the landscape around the cabin to sort of proxy what had been thick green vegetation.

Following all of these events, I managed to spin off a small piece of the company I had been working for and started my own software development company. Now I was able to stay home full time, what a wonderful break from commuting! My wife landed a job with one of the small businesses in The Village, so we didn't have to travel outside our rural retreat accept for the occasional trek to the city for groceries and other necessities. We had much more time to spend together which allowed us to keep up with the chores of maintaining the lifestyle I loved so much.

A Near Miss

Following the November wildfire, we became acutely sensitive anytime we heard an orbiting helicopter. Such was the case on a late October morning a couple of years later. Another wildfire had erupted about ten miles as a crow flies from our cabin. Of course by now we were far better prepared for evacuation and had a plan in place. The first item on the agenda was to turn on the news to find out specifics. Once we figured out the location and from which direction the fire was traveling, we determined the best course of action would be to turn the cars facing out of the drive way and load them with our pictures, clothing, computers, and files just in case. Wildfires, depending on the size and conditions, can literally generate their own weather, predicting the direction of the burn and the speed at which it is moving is extremely difficult if not impossible at times.

Burning embers can soar for miles causing spot fires to break out. While I kept an ear to the TV and an eye on the smoke, I noticed a group of high school aged kids walking into the park towards the location of the fire. I called out to them asking where they were going and why. "We're going to look at the fire" one of group responded. I told them if the wind shifts they might not be able to out run it. By the end of the day the fire had passed within a couple of miles and one ridge over from our canyon thus marking another end to high anxiety.

Chapter 4 Evaluating the Basics

So far I have written about my experiences with some pretty dicey events. My purpose is not to discourage pursuing a rural lifestyle; rather it is intended to provide you with a detailed look at a very large picture as it pertains to rural living. I realize the same events can happen in the city, but as I have mentioned, services can be much farther away thus significantly increasing the response time in the event of an emergency. The name of the game is to diminish risk as much as possible. In this chapter I will discuss many of the less major considerations for preparing for cabin living in a rural environment with the intent of inducing comfort and simplicity.

Beware the Handyman's Dream

Whether you are planning to purchase or you are fortunate enough to rent a cabin in the country, you've no doubt seen the phase "handyman's dream" used as a selling point to push the product. "Fixer upper", "quaint", "charming", and "cozy" are a few more terms which raise a red flag for me as well. Cabins in rural areas are high maintenance propositions. Cabins tend to be more exposed to the elements, are often repaired by previous occupants with no qualified experience, or simply neglected altogether. My cabin fits all of these descriptions yet I was willing to endure certain inconveniences because of the location.

The most obnoxious problem was the never ending siege by field rats and mice (Under "Know Your Fauna" I discuss how to combat the problem in an eco-friendly way). For every hole I stuffed with steel wool and patched with mud ("mud" is actually a term for spackle) inside and out, yet another hole would appear. Rodent's ability to chew through seemingly anything is truly remarkable if not downright frustrating. On one occasion, rats had chewed through a part of the wiring harness on my motorcycle. I had to buy and install a new harness. Imagine if they chewed through the electrical system of my car or truck. The repair could be very costly which is why I became so vigilant in eliminating these critters. At least the field vermin in the country are not as bad as dealing with sewer rats of the city.

Second to rodents are roof leaks. I'd have a roofer come out and fix the latest leaks only to find a few more the next time it rained. Walking on the roof hastens damage; I recommend accessing the roof only for repairs to the roof itself. Use a ladder to clear fallen leaves and limbs, and to clean the stove pipe filter.

Lastly was the plumbing. Most of the outdoor plumbing at my cabin was not properly insulated and not buried deep enough to prevent freezing at least a few times each winter. But it didn't matter what season it was, pin hole leaks would sprout year round.

Cabins must be inspected carefully if you want to avoid any of these inconveniences. For example: What, if any, wood siding is rotting particularly if the siding extends below ground level? Is the exhaust pipe for the stove properly sealed from leakage through the roof? And, don't forget to flush the toilet to test the septic system!

Cabin Fever?

While the definitions of "Cabin Fever" includes primarily claustrophobia (fear of cramped quarters), I associate cabin fever (although erroneously), more with agoraphobia which is a fear of vast open spaces, certain social interaction, or crowded places such as malls or stadiums. Why do I bring this subject up? Because this is a guide about cabin living and while somewhat out of the scope of all of the physical attributes of cabin living, there are potential mental aspects as well. Aside from becoming accustomed and experienced to day to day cabin living and perhaps the occasional stress test provided by the elements, there is one other component which I must address.

If you are in the process of looking for or have already just moved in to your dream cabin, consider what cabin living might be like a year, three years, or more from now. My own personal experience with regards to a "mental" state of mind after nearly 20 years of relatively isolated cabin living ultimately developed into acquiring parts of agoraphobia, namely disdain for large crowds and certain social situations. I am not a qualified physician or psychologist; I can only surmise that living alone for many years followed by sharing my cabin lifestyle with my new wife changed the way I look at the suburban environment: forever. Later in this guide I describe having to leave my "security blanket" after so many years.

Cistern Size, Water Issues

If you have running water from a main, then you are not as likely to consider a cistern for water storage. However, I would consider a cistern for storing water in the event of an emergency such as failure of the water main or other plumbing issues. In addition, I store water in a half dozen six gallon water jugs for portability in case I have to bug out.

Note: don't forget about your water heater. In an emergency, you have a substantial amount of water suitable for drinking stored conveniently in your water heater.

Cistern capacities are all over the board. I have seen some which are several hundred gallons to several thousand gallons. The smaller cisterns are generally for short term emergencies for those on a water main, or for those living part time in their cabin. The size of a larger cistern meant for every day use depends on several parameters:

- How many residents will occupy the cabin?

- Will the cabin be occupied seasonally or year round?

- Are there catch basins or other methods which can add to water storage during the rainy season?

Low flow toilets and the amount of laundry will also factor into how much water is necessary. I have researched estimates of as much as 50 gallons per day per person as a baseline.

Then there is the cost of having the water trucked in. Maintaining a cistern twice the volume of one truck load obviously means another trip for the water truck adding to the cost. The old cistern for my cabin was made of steel and easily stored 1,000 gallons of water. The original plumbing from the cistern to the cabin (shown immediately next to the left arrow) is still in place today. And, to the left of the smaller arrow is one of our neighbors, the bobcat! Unfortunately, he never would let me get any closer when I happened to have a camera handy.

Firewood

I purchase firewood indigenous to, and bought locally in the area where I plan to use it, not only for warming the cabin, but for camping trips as well. Buying firewood sets an example for those who are irresponsible by discouraging picking the forests clean of dead wood, live tree branches, and other plants. Also, bringing firewood from outside the area you plan to use it can introduce foreign plant or insect matter into the local environment and ultimately cause serious damage to the trees around you.

For the cabin, I usually purchase a cord of mix, mostly hard wood which burns hotter and longer. A cord of wood is typically defined as 8 feet long by 4 feet wide, by 4 feet high. And, I have to make sure the wood I purchase contains as part of the mix wood which can be used for tinder and kindling. You'll need every advantage you can get if you have to start a fire in a cold, damp cabin.

The firewood you purchase should be cut to length, preferably no more than two feet. And, unless you plan to split logs, I wouldn't get anything larger than five or six inches in diameter. Select an even variety of sizes; you'll want smaller sizes for starting your fire each night, and a proportionate number of larger pieces as well. This obviously saves having to split and cut firewood which can be an enormous chore. I bought firewood by the cord which is not as expensive as buying smaller quantities. The cord was usually a mix of both soft and hard woods. The soft wood such as pine is easier to start, but burns quickly. Hard wood like oak is more difficult to start and even more difficult to cut and split, but burns longer and hotter.

I don't recommend burning any treated wood such as scrap from a construction site, pallets, or furniture. Treated wood produce fumes which can be toxic and your cabin will be exposed to a certain amount of potential carcinogens. The filter and screen at the top of the exhaust pipe will clog quicker when burning treated wood. The same applies for burning plastic cups, wrapping, and utensils.

Note: if you do have to split and cut larger logs, I recommend having as part of your tool collection a couple different sizes of a splitting axe, sledge hammer, and a wedge.

Freezing pipes, Water Pressure Valve

Although all water pipes should be insulated and buried, there will be the occasional exceptionally cold night where pipes freeze. If you are on a main, the water pressure valve (a water pressure valve is used to "step down" the water pressure from the water main so as not to overload the plumbing in the cabin) may also burst if not properly insulated. In addition to an assortment of lengths and diameters of pipes and other plumbing supplies which I keep on hand, I like the rubber clamps specifically for pin hole leaks caused by freezing pipes. They buy me enough time to get to the hardware store in the event I don't have the right replacement part.

You probably already know about the trick of turning on a faucet to allow a small trickle of water overnight to help keep water pipes from freezing. Running water freezes at a lower temperature than standing water.

I took this concept a bit farther and installed an additional valve at the water main so I could completely drain the water from the pipe between the main and the cabin. I only used this method when I knew the temperatures were going drop significantly.

Heating and "Air Conditioning"

I never used any type of electric heater. I don't consider them safe and they add considerably to whatever the source of electricity is (in particular the electric bill if you are on the grid). The only heat in my cabin was a cast iron wood burning stove and it did a great job. The stove was located in the corner of the living room basically the center of the cabin. I was never able to date the stove, but I wouldn't be surprised if it was manufactured as far back as the 1920's. The dimensions of the stove were about 18 inches high, 18 inches wide, and about 3 feet deep.

The stove had cast iron legs which kept if off the floor by about 6 inches. In fact, a 6 by 6 foot area was covered with cinder blocks turned on their side upon which the stove was placed (red arrow below). The cabin floor was wood, so this extra protection was absolutely necessary. The exhaust pipe was perhaps 10 inches in diameter and extended from the rear of the stove through the roof of the cabin.

At the top of the exhaust pipe was a cover preventing rain and leaves from entering, while helping to secure a wire mesh screen around the diameter of the pipe immediately below. It is extremely important to make sure a filter is always in place to prevent burning embers from escaping and starting a wildfire.

It is also important to keep any type of filter clean to allow all smoke to exit the stove through the exhaust pipe. Otherwise, smoke will likely back out inside the cabin and it can take quite awhile to purge the smoke back outside. The exhaust pipe topped by the filter and filter cover is pictured here to the right of the red arrow:

At the front of the stove there was obviously a cast iron door which was always closed, but just as important was the cast iron "tray" which slid in and out such that the stove could be completely sealed off or opened a few inches to allow more heat into the cabin. The tray acted as a thermostat and was highly affective. The doors to the kitchen, bath, and bedrooms further served to control precious heat on cold nights. In addition, the top of the stove was flat and suitable for cooking. I used it occasionally to boil water to raise humidity.

The three most important tools for maintaining a wood burning stove are a steel brush for keeping the filter clean, an ash can, and a small steel shovel. I could burn full time for about two days before I had to the empty ash out of the stove. I'm sure I don't have to point out that all hot ash should be put completely out before disposing it.

As for air conditioning, it was non-existent in terms of a real air conditioning unit complete with a compressor and thermostat. Hot days meant cooling off in the old wooden "hot tub" filled with cold water. Mounting window fans in the windows such that airflow is pushed outside allows a nice cross breeze through the cabin when the hot weather begins to subside for the evening. Window fans blowing outside also means you won't have a bunch of stuff flying around in the inside!

Generator/Solar

Generators are short term solutions in the event the electricity goes out. Although I have used generators, I don't care for the noise (newer models are much quieter though), the exhaust, and I don't like to store gasoline. If your cabin has a nicely exposed south facing roof and you can afford it, solar would be my choice. I was lucky to be close to the main power lines for the area, but close to a quarter mile of line had to be strung to reach my cabin. And there's no guarantee against problems even with the power company. Every major storm, particularly electrical storms, brought down some part of the local grid and sometimes took up to a week to restore. This is another reason to be properly prepared in case any of these options fail. The following picture shows the view of the cliff top from the backroom of the cabin. Many times lightning would strike the top of this cliff sending a resounding boom throughout the canyon!

The elevation of our cliff is about 500 feet. Note the shear drop from the top to about half way down.

Groceries

It is likely the closest general store will be fairly expensive to shop at. Smaller stores have less room for inventory and must pay more for smaller quantities of goods. That additional cost is passed on to the consumer by higher prices. Use the local store for emergencies. When making a trip to the city, stock up on provisions based on how much you can store at home.

Laundry

In keeping with water conservation, we washed mostly large loads using cold water only to save propane. I strung up a clothesline to hang wet laundry to dry. The freshness of laundry hung out to dry in the clean air was simply amazing. The dryer was used only to soften the laundry which had been hung out to dry.

Mail

The U.S. Postal Service will continue to downsize for the unforeseen future. Find out specifically how mail delivery to the cabin you are considering living in is achieved. Your cabin may be on a rural route where you actually have your own mailbox, there might be a "gang box" (a kiosk containing many separate mailboxes) installed in a centralized location serving the surrounding area, or you may be required to rent a Post Office Box.

Pets

The best way I can illustrate caring for pets in a rural area is unfortunately by an all too often occurrence of "Lost Pet" signs posted on telephone poles around the neighborhood. We always knew when we had a new neighbor because within a month of moving in they would lose a pet. It is sad these folks didn't do their homework; you can't let your pets run freely outside of the cabin even in a fenced in area. The exceptions might be larger dogs, but I have read articles about mountain lions dragging 100 pound German Sheppard's over a six foot high cinder block wall.

Cats, smaller dogs, and even children are fair game for coyotes, hawks, owls, and bobcats. Remember that you are "guests" in their territory, not the other way around. I recall an incident in the fashionable suburbs near Malibu, California where an actress was watching her two Chihuahuas playing in her front yard when all of a sudden a couple of hawks swooped in and grabbed her little dogs never to be seen again.

For the most part, coyotes, owls, and the big cats are nocturnal and was a rare occasion that I ever saw one in broad daylight. I woke often in the middle of the night to the shrieking of a pack of coyotes which had surrounded their prey. In only a minute or two, it was all over.

In a somewhat different subject regarding pets is the unfortunate occurrences of folks dumping their pets in rural areas. I "adopted" those which showed up on my porch until I could find a permanent home for them. Too bad I was never able to catch any of the perpetrators.

Phone, Internet

In my opinion, if there is no cell service in your area the best option is a land line if your cabin is close enough to a telephone company junction box. If you can get Internet access, then "Voice Over IP" (telephone over the Internet) is another option and is much less expensive than the traditional telephone company land line. I also keep a Citizen's Band (CB) radio handy just in case. CB's channel 9 is reserved for and is monitored by law enforcement agencies for emergencies. Of course any of these options will be determined by the location of your cabin.

Propane

If your cabin is not within distance of a natural gas main, the alternative will likely be propane. The size of the propane tank should be dependent on how much is used during some certain amount of time. For example, I only used propane for cooking and the water heater (for my wife and myself); 50 gallons per month was about average. Consider a larger propane tank if there are more people living in the cabin, if a clothes dryer is to be used, if propane is to be used for heat, or if you feel more comfortable having a larger supply on hand. And, check the gauge regularly to make sure you're not running low. Running out of propane means you will have to relight the pilots for older stoves and water heaters.

Note: propane burns hotter than natural gas. You may find you will have to adjust your cooking skills a bit to keep from burning food during cooking.

Septic Systems

It's a good bet that if your cabin is rural, you will be using a septic system. The goal of maximum comfort assumes you are well stocked with equipment, provisions, and firewood for daily living or any hunker down event. That said, your septic system then becomes the most important component of comfortable rural cabin living. Making trips to the outhouse at 2:00am in cold rainy weather should be reserved for camping trips and not part of cabin living. I encourage you to research your septic system as to what is actually disposed through the septic system. In addition to the obvious, what about used water from the kitchen and bathroom sink, and the bath and shower? Regardless of what waste is disposed of, it is imperative that nothing which cannot be broken down organically enter the system.

Items such as paper towels, cotton swaps, and tampons can not only impede the natural process of eliminating by-products in the septic system, they can also clog any of the lines to the septic tank. All sinks, bathtubs, and showers must have strainers fine enough to keep all food, soap chips, and hair from going down the drain. Also, garbage disposals in the kitchen sink should not considered safe for use for a septic system. I recommend using biodegradable soap, but check with an expert on septic maintenance on what is best to use.

As you have already read back in chapter 3, I have a fair amount of experience repairing septic failures. Of course you don't have do it yourself if you can afford several thousand dollars to hire a contractor. Either way, it's a huge pain in the neck.

Leach Locations

Leach lines allow the transfer of material in the septic tank to what is referred to as a leach field. A leach field contains a collection of pipes which are perforated and are usually set in gravel and buried well below the ground surface allowing organic material to disperse and liquid to percolate. Damage to leach lines of leach fields should be evaluated and repaired by a professional.

Line Locations

Knowing where the location of the lines from the cabin to the tank can come in handy in the event of a clog or a break in the pipe. Once again, the option is yours; do it yourself or hire a plumber at a hundred bucks an hour. If you decide to dig down to the line in question, your choices are to begin at where the line enters the cabin, or begin digging where the line enters the septic tank and in either case trench back to the break. You will know soon enough when you get close to the break.

The following picture shows the amount of trenching necessary to locate a break in my line. The trench was about four feet by about a foot wide. The yellow thirty foot measuring tape gives you an idea of how far the tank is buried from the cabin. The sandbags were in place to keep the trenches from filling up before repairs could be made.

The picture below shows a heavy duty flexible line used to repair a break in the PVC. The break was caused by tree roots which had grown large enough to crush the PVC against the compacted ground. I used large steel clamps to secure each end of the flexible line. I affected this repair soon after I moved into the cabin. This repair remained in perfect condition fifteen years later when I had to dig it all up again.

Older systems will have pipe made of clay while newer systems will have PVC piping. Consult a professional on the proper way to repair a broken septic line.

Tank Location

There are several reasons why you should know exactly where the septic tank is located, particularly the covers. If you know where the covers are located, chances are it will only take you an hour or so to dig up the surrounding soil (depending on how far down you must dig to expose the covers). Keep the area where the covers reside easily accessible. Never store heavy equipment or park a vehicle over the septic tank or cover area. This picture shows what the covers look like when exposed. Note that they are only a few feet deep.

Note: knowing leach, line, and tank locations is also very important if you ever need to have heavy trucks or tractors perform any work in or around your cabin. Parking vehicles, especially heavy vehicles, can collapse any part of the system rendering the entire system useless.

Shown here is the leach side of the tank. I described back in chapter 3 how an earthquake offset the septic tank by about a foot. I repaired the gap by installing a couple of elbow fittings:

Maintenance

A septic tank likely will not have to be pumped more than a few times during the life of the tank which, if properly maintained, can last a half century. Consult a septic system professional for instructions on the type of enzymes to be used (if any), how often, and how to apply enzymes. Depending on the size of the tank and how much and how often material is discharged from the cabin plumbing will determine how often, if at all, enzymes are added to the system. However, if the tank overflows due to flooding or some other system failure, pumping the tank may be necessary. Exposing the covers prior to the arrival of the pumping service will save you a few bucks.

If you suspect a break or obstruction in the line between the cabin and the septic tank, you can seek professional assistance which could set you back some serious cash, or you can attempt to clear it yourself. Breaks in the line are often caused by tree roots growing around the line putting pressure between the line, the roots, and the compacted ground the line is buried in. Obstructions are often caused by non-organic items introduced into the system which get caught in elbow joints or other parts of the line.

If you attempt to clear the line your self, you will need to locate an access point to the line usually somewhere around the base of the cabin behind the toilet. You will need to rent a professional grade snake and know how to use it. Beware, rental yards will charge a small fortune if you break the bit.

Usually an obstruction can be cleared using a snake. If the line has been compromised by roots, or otherwise broken and clogged with soil, you will know upon inspecting the contents on the bit of the snake after reeling it back in. You should be able to recognize whether tree roots or soil is the culprit. In either of these two cases, the pipe will have to be replaced.

Starting a Fire in a Wood Burning Stove

Although I've used a number of methods to start fires, such as flint and steel, and magnesium bars, I am not on a camping trip. The theme is always simple and comfortable. So I use the tried and true fire starting method called lighter fluid. Yeah, it's cheating a bit, but I figure I've put in more than my fair share of time and effort over the years using other fire starting techniques. Before beginning to build your fire, use your knife to shave off strips of wood which can be lit by a match. This is called tinder; a handful should do the trick. Using an axe or hatchet and split a dozen or so pieces about the size of a drinking straw, and maybe a half dozen pieces the size of a road flare.

Note: Did you know a dull knife, axe, or hatchet blade is actually much more dangerous than a sharp one? Tools with dull blades can "bounce" off the wood you are trying to cut causing you to lose control of the tool and increasing your risk for injury. There are many fine guides available showing you how to sharpen and maintain blades for any tool.

Set the axe or hatchet blade with the grain by hitting the wood with the blade while at the same time hitting the wood on a solid surface. Use just enough force to set the blade into the wood. Then you can lift the axe or hatchet with the piece of wood attached (without worrying about your other hand) and hit it against a solid surface. Using this technique precludes you from having to take a full swing of the axe or hatchet at a relatively small target.

The teepee method is the most effective way of starting a fire and requires the least amount of work. If you take the time to set this up right, it will light with one match. Assuming the old ash in your stove is completely burned out use a small steel shovel to empty the ash into an ash can.

Place paper items which would otherwise go to a landfill and use them as tinder at the bottom of the fire pit. Otherwise use the tinder you made as I described above. Begin building your teepee on top of the tinder using the kindling you split. Start with smaller, thinner pieces, followed by yet thicker, longer pieces.

What we're trying to accomplish by doing this, is to allow for enough oxygen to fuel the flame initially. In the picture above, I have purposely exaggerated a bit to illustrate the concept. And, you'll have to imagine the teepee shown above as it would look like in your stove as I was unable to take a suitable picture actually in the wood burning stove. This teepee would probably start with one match; however, you will want to use several more pieces of each size and more kindling to ensure an easy start. Once the kindling is going, gradually add increasingly larger pieces of wood. Challenge yourself and your guests each night to see who can get the fire going using just one match and without using lighter fluid!

Trash

Similar to mail and other services, trash pickup may be handled by any one of several methods. Trash receptacles placed at the end of your driveway on trash day, a neighborhood dumpster placed in a centralized location, incineration (check the local laws and ordinances), or you may have to haul to a dumpsite yourself. Regardless of the method, trash should be secured in steel receptacles to prevent animals from scattering it all over the neighborhood. If you plan to live in bear country, I suggest trash receptacles which can withstand intrusion by hungry bears.

Vehicle Reliability

My vehicles are always well maintained to achieve the best reliability as possible. Having more than one vehicle significantly increases the size of the "safety net" in the event you must leave. And don't leave fuel tanks near empty.

Common Vehicle Maintenance

You already know about the more common tips for saving on wear and tear like making sure you have proper air pressure in your tires and don't let your gas tank run too low as sediment at the bottom could clog fuel lines and fuel injectors.

Read the owners manual for your vehicle. Check what grade of fuel is recommended for your vehicle. Most vehicles don't require high octane fuel; use the grade of fuel the vehicle is designed for. How often do you have the oil changed? It used to be widely accepted that every 3,000 miles you should have the oil changed. Again, refer to your vehicle owners' manual. Many newer vehicles require oil changes about every 7,000 miles.

Check Engine Light

According to a well known automotive data firm, the average vehicle on the road is now over 10 years old, up from about 8 years a decade ago. While maintaining your vehicle is expensive in the short term, proper maintenance can save you thousands in the long term. And, one of the most common indicators of potential problems with your vehicle is the infamous "Check Engine" indicator. Here are the five most common reasons your "Check Engine" light might come on, and what you can expect to pay for the repair, including labor:

1. Faulty Oxygen Flow Sensor

This sensor measures the amount of unburned oxygen in the exhaust and tells the vehicles' computer how much fuel is in the tank. If a faulty sensor is not replaced, the vehicle's gas mileage could drop. Replacing a faulty sensor may cost as much as $200. Not replacing it could cost much more in wasted fuel.

2. Malfunctioning Mass Air Flow Sensor

This sensor measures the amount of air supplied to the engine, which determines how much fuel should be delivered. When it malfunctions, it can result in a loss of power to the car, surges during acceleration and a decrease in fuel economy. It can cost as much as $350 to fix.

3. Misfiring Spark Plugs

Misfiring spark plugs can affect engine performance and fuel economy and may also damage the catalytic converter. You can replace spark plugs yourself for as little as $20 or pay as much or more than $200 for a technician to do it.

4. Loose or Missing Gas Cap

This is my favorite one because I've fixed this myself on several occasions. Try filling the fuel tank to capacity, tighten the gas cap, and give it a couple of days to see if the check engine light turns off. If not, replace the gas cap entirely which shouldn't cost more than perhaps $20. Again, fill the tank to capacity and give it a few days, maybe a week, to see if the light goes out.

5. Broken Catalytic Converter

This one is the worst news by far since a new catalytic converter can cost several thousand dollars to replace. The catalytic converter is usually made of a precious metal such as platinum which converts harmful gases to less harmful emissions. Catalytic converters generally won't fail unless a related part, such as a spark plug, fails. Yet another good reason to properly maintain your vehicle.

Here's another tip, especially if you own a newer more expensive vehicle: Take your vehicle to a muffler shop and have them "tack" each end of the catalytic converter. "Tacking" means spot weld a few places around the muffler clamps. This will help prevent thieves from stealing your catalytic converter. Remember, they are made of platinum, which can be worth as much or more than gold by the ounce.

Vehicle Suitability

Depending on how rural you plan to live will probably have an impact of the type of vehicle(s) you may want to consider. In my situation, I had a camper for both vacationing and bugging out in an emergency. In addition, I also had a four wheel drive truck for the occasional creek crossings, pulling stranded neighbors out of flooded roadways, and sometimes just to get out of my own driveway after a downpour turned it to mud. On several occasions, large oak trees fell across the driveway. Unfortunately, these trees sustained too much damage from the fire and eventually succumbed from infection. I chained up the fallen tree to the truck and was able to easily pull it out of the way. But, after cutting the trees to stove lengths, splitting, and seasoning, oak is my favorite wood to burn and one tree lasted almost one winter season.

Does a Falling Tree in the Forest Make Noise?

By the way, I happened to be in my living room one warm summer afternoon when I heard a gentle "whoosh" outside. It was then I new for fact that falling trees in the forest do make noise! The amazing part was how little noise it actually made. Had I been only a few hundred yards away, I might not have heard it.

A Couple of Rescue Stories

While we're sort of on the subject, and for your entertainment, the following are a couple of real stories where I was able to pull folks out of a sticky situation. Among my many off road adventures, pulling folks out of dicey situations are the most challenging, gratifying, and thrilling out of all the rest of the obstacles. Translation – Fun!

Over the Cliff (Almost)

One memorable occasion while out for a day trip with my wife, we had ventured off the main highway several miles to the end of a campground in the local mountains. It was late fall at about 6,000 feet and the sun was about to go down. This area is well known for nighttime temperatures often dropping into the teens or lower that time of the year. I only wanted to explore the campground in detail in case it might be a place I would want to go for an overnight camping trip.

At the end of the campground in the very last camp spot we spotted a couple perhaps in their early thirties. There was no immediate sign of a vehicle, cooler, picnic basket, or any other equipment. The scene obviously didn't add up so I stopped and inquired if they needed any assistance. And they sure did. Somehow the woman had driven their car through the barrier of the parking area and over the embankment about twenty feet. So far they were fortunate because the car had stopped just before a drop off into a steep canyon several hundred feet farther down. And again fortunately for them I had a heavy chain with hooks on either end about 20 feet long for towing. The tricky part was nosing my truck right to the edge such that I could get close enough to the car without going over the edge myself.

Without an inch to spare, I hooked up the front of my truck to the rear of their car. I engaged my truck into compound low four wheel drive. The fact that I nosed in front first meant that the engine, front differential, and transfer case were all weight which would help give me traction. I always ease the throttle at first to check for traction, to make sure the chain isn't going to release, and to minimize damage to either vehicle. Giving it a little more gas and watching my tachometer, I eased the car back up onto the level parking area. That couple couldn't have been happier. I never inquired as to how she managed to drive the car over the embankment and nearly five hundred feet over a cliff, I could see they had already been extremely stressed and were now very much relieved. I let it go at that; we said goodbye and all went on our way.

Extra Care When Visiting the Desert

My wife and I were on an extended exploration trip through the southern most part of California along the Mexican border. It was the middle of summer and well over one hundred degrees. Temperatures have known to reach one hundred fifteen degrees and higher in that region which is defined as "low" desert. We were traveling the main highway looking for a turnoff to do some off road site seeing in the State Park when we passed a station wagon up to its axle in the sandy shoulder. As we turned around and pulled up behind the stuck vehicle, we met a family of four, the two kids were perhaps in their early teens, mom was visibly upset, and dad was panicking – foot on the gas all the way while slamming the transmission back and forth from forward to reverse only to dig himself even deeper into the soft sand.

I managed to calm everyone down and explained what I was going to do, and nobody disagreed. I chained up his rear axle to a hard point on the front of my truck. As always, I engaged the four wheel drive and put the transmission into compound low, gave a little gas to make sure the hookup was solid. I had to give this one a bunch of throttle because all four of my wheels were digging in at the same time I was pulling him out. Once out of his hole, I had to drag him past the holes I created and then back onto pavement. I learned a valuable lesson on this particular event – never let the other driver turn his engine on, take the keys if you have to. Once he had traction, he almost backed into me. That wouldn't have been so bad, but I shudder to think about what else might go wrong if there are too many cooks in the kitchen at the same time. But no harm done, and a very relieved family were on their way again. Oh, I should mention that right in front of where he got stuck was a sign posted "Soft Shoulder".

The Dam

"The Dam" was short for a reservoir we frequented often in the spring and early summer months before the creek dried up. Most of the area was designated for off road use but I favored off-roading upstream where I could enjoy my favorite pool. On this outing, my wife and I had spent the day swimming and sunning in peace and quiet and were just getting ready to leave. The pool was easily six feet deep and I had caught a limit of trout earlier that afternoon. So, I guess this was as good a time as any for the arrival of some good ole' boys driving a mid size four wheel drive pickup truck right down the middle of the creek and heading to the pool we had just spent the day at. I figured they knew what they were doing so we just got out of way and watched.

To my amazement, they drove nose first right into the deepest part of the pool. The engine quit and the cab instantly filled up with water. The driver and passenger had to exit out the windows. At least the rear of the truck bed was still exposed. It soon became clear these guys had way too much to drink but that didn't hinder them from asking me for an assist. I told him I would try, but it wasn't looking too good for them and I wasn't about to get stuck too.

My only option was to maneuver up the creek, turn around, and as usual try to nose my front end as close to the other vehicle without getting stuck myself. This time it was much trickier because I little room from side to side in a narrow channel to work with and I was sitting all the way in the creek on slippery rock. At least I didn't have to worry about him starting his engine. This time I had to rock his truck back and forth to gain some momentum because all four of my tires were spinning. I had him out in about twenty minutes though. Surprisingly, and very much unlike so many others I have assisted, he asked me how much I wanted for the help. I replied "what do you have in the cooler?" We agreed on giving me a cold six pack which I figured he didn't need anyway. I stuck around for a while longer until he got his truck started.

Summary

I carry three types of towline each for a different purpose:

1) A 20 foot length of chain with hooks on either end for heavier vehicles which I can get close to.

2) About a 30 foot length of 3/8 inch cable, again with hooks on either end if I can't get as close.

3) A 15 foot nylon towline rated for 6,000 pounds for lighter vehicles and if I need the flexibility of rope versus cable.

In any situation where I am pulling other vehicles out of various situations, everyone must be well out of the way and protected by standing behind large trees or boulders. If any of the towlines should fail, there is easily enough kinetic energy to sever small trees, parts of the vehicles, or, well let's not get into that. I've had hundreds of occasions both being pulled out of situations and doing my share, call it payback, to help others by pulling them out of dicey conditions. Learning by experience can be painful. You can just as easily put yourself at risk as much as the fellow you are trying to help. Use common sense, and never be shy about asking questions from someone who has experience.

Water Heater

If you are on propane, make sure the water heater is rated for the use of propane. Just like natural gas, propane does not naturally contain an odor. And like natural gas, propane is induced with an additive before it's available for distribution. The additive smells somewhat like rotten eggs allowing any leaks or unlit pilots to be detected. My water heater was situated outside the cabin in an enclosure designed specifically for a water heater. I also installed a water heater cover for added insulation. Adjusting the temperature depending on the season helped conserve propane (it's not cheap!). In fact, during hotter weather, showering outside was mandatory!

Important Note: before lighting any pilots, be sure that all propane has dissipated from inside the cabin. Leave the oven door open and take the pilot access cover off of the water heater to allow the fumes to escape. Lighting a match while there are still fumes about can cause an explosion.

Tip: I use fireplace matches for lighting the pilot on the water heater and hard to reach pilots. Fireplace matches are much longer and easier to reach the pilot. If you don't have fireplace matches, tape a clothespin to the end of a straightened out clothes hanger wire. Light a kitchen match, insert in the clothes pin, and light the pilot.

Chapter 5 Preparation, Prevention and Property Maintenance

Preparation

Keeping tabs on the weather in a rural setting must be part of daily living. At least at my cabin it was, and it didn't matter what day of the year. I recommend keeping a source for weather broadcasts and other potential threats whether it's a TV or just a simple portable radio. I had to know as far ahead of time of any storms coming my way (especially after the fire) so I could make sure all my preparations were in place. I checked for breaches in the sandbags, covered the firewood, and double checked flashlights just to name a few.

Check the Weather, 40% Chance of Rain?

The following is a little research I have done to explain forecasted chances of rain and what they mean. From this information I can attempt to extrapolate the severity of the weather and get some idea of what to expect in my area.

Ever wonder what the weather forecasters mean by a "40% chance" of rain? Will it rain 40% of the time? Will it rain over 40% of the area? Forecasts issued by the National Weather Service typically include a Probability of precipitation (PoP) declaration which is expressed as the "chance of rain" or "chance of precipitation". The PoP describes the chance of precipitation occurring at any selected location in a given area. How is PoP calculated? Mathematically, PoP is defined as follows:

PoP = C x A where C is equal to the confidence that precipitation will occur somewhere in the forecast area, and where A is equal to the percent of the area that will receive measureable precipitation, if there is any precipitation at all. Using a 40% chance as an example, if the forecaster expects precipitation to occur at a 100% level of confidence, and expects 40% of a given area receiving measurable rain, then PoP = C x A or "1" times ".4" equaling .4 or 40%.

However, most of the time forecasts are expressed as a combination of degree of confidence and area coverage. If the level of confidence is only 50% that measurable rain will occur over 80% of the area, the PoP is 40%, or PoP = .5 x .8 which equals .4 or 40%. In either event, the correct way to interpret the forecast is: there is a 40% chance that rain will occur at any given point in the area.

Or, in my opinion, a 40% chance of rain means a 100% chance of rain over 40% of a given area. I think my definition is easier to understand, and it errors on the side of being better prepared. Besides, you might as well just use a dart board to predict the weather and be prepared for anything.

Fire Season and the Santa Ana Winds

The infamous Santa Ana winds of the Southwest can pack punches well beyond category 1 hurricane force winds, though usually gusts of forty to fifty miles an hour are more common. Peak times of the year for the Santa Ana winds where my cabin is located are generally late summer and early fall although the phenomenon can occur any time during the year.

The Santa Ana winds are caused by a massive high pressure system which envelops much of Utah and Nevada pushing hot air through parts of California. In addition to the high winds and warmer temperatures, humidity can drop below double digits. Santa Ana conditions are largely responsible for the propagation of wild fires.

The definition of "fire season" changed with the wildfire I described in an earlier chapter which nearly burned down our cabin. You either cannot define fire season or define it as all year round. Combined with drought conditions, a defensive posture must be taken to lessen the risk of loss of life and property from wildfire. And it doesn't hurt to be extra vigilant for visitors ignorant of the situation. I once caught some visitors parked off the side of the road near our cabin smoking and flicking their ash directly into dry brush. Although they didn't speak English and I had no clue what they were saying, I still got the point across. Talk about zero common sense. This was but just one of many times I have had to chase down idiots for smoking in a clearly marking no smoking area due to high fire danger.

Prevention and Property Maintenance

Brush Clearance

The single most effective preventative measure against loss from wildfire is brush clearance. Depending on your location there may be different requirements, some even a little too extreme. Several hundred feet around any structure is typical while just how close you cut to ground cover or top soil is usually controversial. Denuding large portions of land can be dangerous in flood conditions, so it's best to contact local authorities for guidelines. I clear about 300 to 400 feet around my cabin, but I leave several inches of ground cover in place.

Fire Resistant Roofs and Siding

Yet another key defense against being a victim of wildfire is the material the cabin roof is made of. All I can suggest (remember, I am not a licensed contractor and not qualified to recommend specifics on construction topics) is to consult a qualified construction consultant to evaluate the roof of your cabin as it pertains to resistance against flame and embers. And I know nobody wants to anyone to utter "siding" as in something like aluminum, but inquire about your options with a qualified construction consultant. Unfortunately for our cabin, the roof was barely passable as fire resistant while the siding was all shake.

Flying Embers

There is one more preventative measure which there really is no excuse for not observing. Red hot embers from a wildfire can travel miles setting off spot fires which potentially can grow into major wildfires of their own. Closing off all openings to attics, basements, crawlspaces, and outbuildings will prevent flying embers from entering the stucture. Keep rain gutters and anywhere an ember could get caught clear of debris which otherwise might allow ignition.

While there are never any 100% guarantees these measures will always protect lives and property, being prepared and deploying prevention techniques as I have experienced and described can increase the chances considerably. If nothing else, awareness and routine maintenance could buy precious seconds which could mean the difference between survival and disaster.

Non-Indigenous Trees, Tree Trimming

One of the more hazardous issues when it comes to landscaping is the planting of trees which are not native to the area. My experience with rural living has shown me that most cabin dwellers don't really "landscape; rather they covet all trees, shrubs, and plants which are native to where they live. Indigenous flora is more suitable for the environment. For example, succulents are better suited to the harsh desert environment while Live Oaks are hardy trees better capable of surviving a wild fire.

Pine trees of course are a symbol of our national parks and forests. While they thrive throughout a vast area of our country, there are areas of particularly high fire danger which are not suitable for the soft, sappy, quick igniting pine tree. Obviously, if your cabin is in the forest populated with pines, just be extra aware of how much more combustible these trees are compared to others. The area around my cabin has pine trees; however, those closest didn't make it through the fire so that issue remedied itself over time.

Keeping trees trimmed of most dead branches is another strategy for decreasing fire danger. I always emphasize my judgment against excessive unnecessary clearing. There must be something left to act as mulch to allow the soil to regenerate and continue the natural cycle of growth. The trimming of trees may be within the jurisdiction of your county or township so you'll want to do some research. The area where my cabin is located has extremely strict rules regarding the trimming or cutting down of any Live Oak. Country inspectors must arrive on the property for a personal inspection prior to issuing the required permit for any work performed on a Live Oak.

For example, only dead branches under four inches in diameter may be cut down and only dead branches not exceeding one inch in diameter and only up to eight feet above ground may be trimmed. As far as my neighbors live away from my cabin, I can assure you they would be right on top of me at the first sound of a chainsaw!

Upon securing a permit, I recommend hiring a licensed and bonded tree trimmer to do the job. All it takes is one mistake and you could have a sizeable tree in your living room. My brother-in-law has over 25 years or experience in this line of work and I have hired him on a couple of occasions (upon getting my permit, of course!). My cabin sits along a hillside which adds greatly to the care which must be taken when cutting larger limbs is necessary. He uses large block and tackle and heavy rope to secure each section of the branch to be cut with the other end of the rope tied off to stakes driven several feet into the ground. Other lengths of heavy rope are also secured to the section of the limb to be cut and dropped to crewmen on the ground to "steer" the section of limb away from the cabin and any other structures within the immediate area. It's quite a site to see a couple of guys each with a couple of different sized chainsaws attached to their waist belt working forty feet or more off the ground.

Shown in this next picture is a large dead tree dangerously angled over the center of the cabin which I had removed upon receiving permission from the county. Note the extensive "canopy" of the many trees surrounding the cabin:

Smoke Detectors

No doubt you have already heard enough about the
importance of installing smoke detectors and of course
changing the batteries once a year or so. But cabin living in
an area of high fire risk and the fact I used a wood burning
stove made smoke detectors mandatory. I mentioned early
on how I set a few outside upon arriving home after a major
wildfire had scorched all of the surrounding land. Well, I
left those smoke detectors outside permanently in addition
to installing several more inside the cabin. And I highly
recommend the type which also alerts you to excessive
carbon monoxide.

Chapter 6 Emergency Preparedness

Design a Plan

One of my favorite hobbies is camping. I have gone camping since I was eleven years old, and have over forty years experience including backpacking the Sierra Nevada Mountains in California and other areas in the Northwest, primitive camping in the Mojave desert, to casual camping at my favorite developed campgrounds along the many lakes and rivers within a few hours drive from where I live. I have assembled and refined my camping equipment to serve me year round and in virtually every environment within a few days drive from my cabin. As it turns out, all of my equipment, for example, propane lanterns, propane stoves, all season tents and sleeping bags, and reserve provisions I keep for my trips all do "double duty" in the event of an emergency. Appendix B includes a list of items I believe are essential to maintain in the event of an emergency.

Emergency preparedness is designed to increase the chances of survival by developing a plan which best fits your particular circumstances. Because I currently reside in California, my primary concerns are earthquakes, floods, and wildfires. Since I have considerable experience with what to do in the event of a major earthquake, flood, or wildfire, I have focused my emergency preparedness plan based on these specific experiences. The occurrence of a major quake or flood likely means having to "hunker down" in a given location for an extended period of time.

The onset of a wildfire typically means evacuation. My emergency preparedness plan isn't necessarily based on any one specific natural event, rather my plan applies to situations where you either must survive in one location or you must evacuate. If evacuation is in order, know all possible ways out of your area. Your driveway could be a potential bottle neck if it represents one way out to the highway. Once at the highway, you have two directions to choose from. And then? It always comes down to the situation at hand. But know all the options including back roads and trails.

Safe storage of emergency preparedness items is essential. Equipment and provisions for emergencies are not going to do much good if they are stored in an outbuilding that burns down or washes away. I am not an expert in natural disasters; I can only recommend the use of common sense and instinct as to how you approach this strategic part of your plan. I store equipment and provisions in different locations around the property so I increase my chances that at least some of it will survive. But, I store in such a way so as not to impede the process of packing my emergency items in the event I must evacuate quickly.

In addition to preparing for an emergency for your home, what about when you're not at home? Since I go camping quite often, my vehicle is always already provisioned with many basic necessities. I carry a small duffle bag with a bath towel, change of clothes, extra pair of light weight shoes, and toiletries. I also pack a couple gallons of water, some canned food, granola bars, and other non-perishable food. Don't forget to pack a can opener too! And just like at home, you should rotate out non-perishables based on expire dates. I always have a heavy coat in the trunk year-round, and during the winter I even throw in a sleeping bag – just in case.

Earthquake Country

While you may not know it, earthquakes are not exclusive to California or the West Coast. Earthquakes have been known to occur in virtually all areas of the United States at one time or another. It just so happens California, and the West Coast in general, lie on fault lines known to be more active, thus producing more frequent quakes of greater magnitude, in turn potentially causing more damage. I have experienced two of the larger earthquakes in California over the past forty years; both were about 6.5 on the Richter scale. I can tell you these were frightening, caused billions of dollars in damage, and many dozens of lives were lost. Yet, these two were small by comparison to those which took place in Japan in April 2011.

There are a few steps you can take to minimize damage and increase the chances of avoiding injury – or worse when preparing for an earthquake. First, and foremost, never run outside. Aside from fire caused by earthquakes, most injuries and deaths occur from debris such as glass and masonry becoming detached from buildings as a result of the shaking. The family plan should be to get under a heavy desk or table and hold on. If you can't make it under such cover, a doorway would be my next choice. I always keep a flashlight and spare pair of shoes next to my bed even though it's not likely I will have enough time to grab them in the event of a larger tremor. I remember as a child how I only had enough time to run for the doorway and how difficult it was to cling to the doorway to keep from being thrown about much like a ship in a storm at sea.

Find out where the shutoff valves to the natural gas (or propane tank) and water are, and know how to shut them off. Know where and how to shut off the electricity to your home. After the initial shock has ended, I recommend shutting everything down regardless of whether they appear to need to be or not. Then inspect your home for any problems with the foundation, walls, roof, and chimney. Next, sweep your immediate neighborhood for any signs of fire, downed power lines, and gas leaks.

Assess your immediate situation with emphasis on what you will require from your emergency preparedness kit and move your family and provisions to a safe location if necessary. The point here is earthquakes are followed by "aftershocks". Aftershocks are typically not as powerful as the initial earthquake, but a 6.5 quake can produce a 6.0 aftershock which can result in additional considerate damage. Assume there will be aftershocks in the coming hours and days.

I don't have any heavy items such as large picture frames hanging on my walls. Instead, I encourage hanging posters in light frames, or hanging tapestry. Same goes for TV sets, they should be free standing and secured to a stud in the wall not only reducing risk of injury during a shaker, but also keeping them from falling on children, or me for that matter.

I also recommend strapping free standing book shelves to studs, and use museum wax to secure vases and other knick knacks to the shelves themselves. Safety locks designed to keep toddlers out of kitchen and bathroom drawers are ideal for cabinets. You might lose all your glass, but at least you lessen the chance the glass will fly all over your floors. This is all quite a bit of work, but Murphy's Law says that if you do it, you'll never need it. Let's hope so.

Contrary to what some folks believe, earthquakes don't cause huge crevasses which open up and swallow everything in sight. Rather, they can cause water mains to break which in turn can cause sink holes. So, if you are on the road at the time a "big" one hits, I recommend pulling over to the side of the road (when it is safe) until it's over. I've seen entire freeway interchanges which had come crashing to the ground looking much like a bombed out city. I would be very cautious about attempting to travel until the authorities have had a chance to inspect the entire surrounding infrastructure.

On a lighter note, I have an interesting (and true) story to tell. It was the day after the Sylmar quake of 1971 when I and some friends decided to go for a hike in the foothills for the afternoon. School was out because of all the damage the earthquake did, so we had a couple of unexpected weeks of free time. I remember clearly around 3:00 in the afternoon we were standing in an open field taking a few minutes rest. There was no wind, not a breeze. But, we could hear what sounded like the wind blowing though the leaves of a large stand of oak trees maybe a hundred yards or so from where we were standing. Then we saw what was causing the trees to shake – the ground was rolling towards us like evenly spaced swells in the ocean perhaps a few feet in height. Then came the violent shaking for maybe ten seconds or so. Turns out we had witnessed first hand the physical shockwave caused by a 6.0 aftershock. I will never forget that afternoon.

Recommended Emergency Equipment

Lanterns

I usually have to break out a lantern once or twice a year during severe weather knocking out power for sometimes days at a time. I like the Coleman dual mantle propane lantern shown below. The top section conveniently screws directly to the propane bottle which also serves as part of the lantern assembly. The bottom of the propane bottle is seated in a plastic base. I always store several extra mantles in my first aid kit.

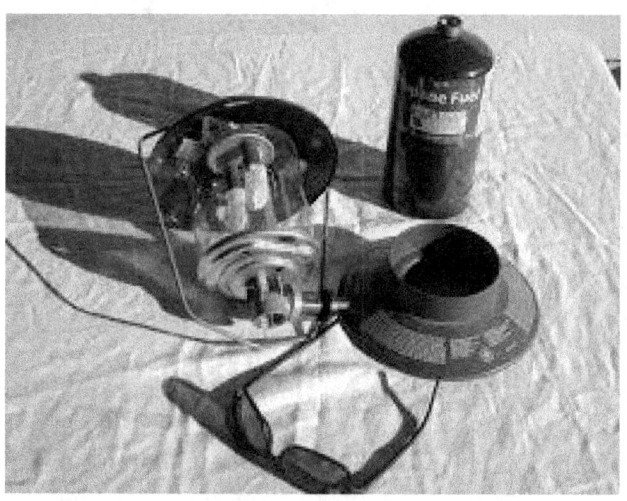

I also store an extra globe just in case. I like this particular model because it uses 16.4 ounce propane bottles, and they are easy pack and store. One bottle averages eight to ten hours of lighting time depending on how high you set the flame. The same type of propane bottle may used with the stove as well.

Replacing the mantle is easy. The mantle is a small sock made of a cloth-like material. It has a draw string at one end. Simply tighten the draw string around the grooved end of the tube carrying the propane from the bottle into the mantle and tie it off. Unfortunately, there's not a lot of room to work with, so I have my wife with smaller hands to do this for me rather than risk damaging a mantle.

Note: I have never allowed the use of candles unless they are fully enclosed within a candle lantern.

Shower, Outdoor

I like to use my outdoor shower during the warmer months to conserve water. And, if some part of the plumbing breaks such that I am unable to use the shower in my cabin, I have a backup. Basically, the outdoor shower is a tent about 5 feet by 5 feet, and about 7 feet high with no floor. Setup the outdoor shower in a low spot, or basin so the water drains away from your cabin.

There is a "shelf" that is actually a net secured inside the shower over your head. This is where you place the shower bladder. The bladder is a flexible plastic or rubber container, similar to a hot water bottle, and is filled with a couple of gallons of water. There is a hose with a shower head which is easily opened and closed when taking your shower.

Place the bladder in the net overhead with the shower head accessible. Depending on the season, you may want to lay the bladders (I suggest having more than one) in direct sunlight to warm the water. Be careful though, this can work too good as the water can heat to scalding hot.

Stove

Although you may be self sufficient with your kitchen stove on propane and your wood burning stove, I recommend a small propane camping stove as a backup if a component of the propane system fails or the wood burn stove becomes inconvenient. Simple is best. I like the two-burner propane model made by Coleman. It's lightweight, easy to setup, has a convenient handle, and folds into the size of a briefcase for easy packing and storage.

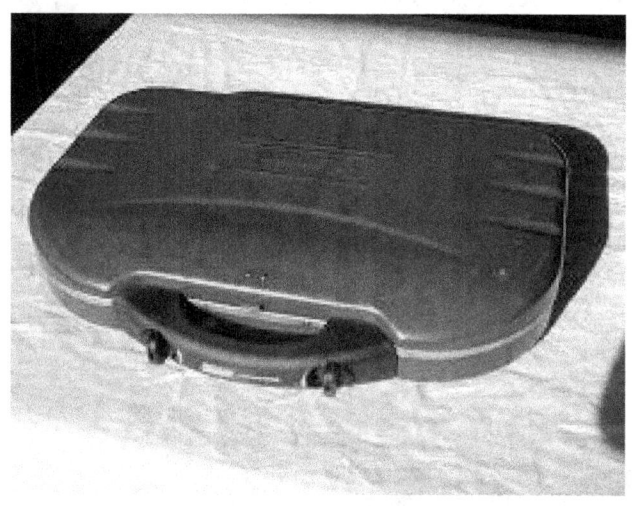

I can take or leave any make or model stove with piezo ignition (also commonly referred to as "matchless" ignition). The concept is great, and when it works it's wonderful. But I have found piezo ignition to be somewhat temperamental. It's not 100% reliable and I'm not sure if it's because of ambient temperature, humidity, altitude, or some combination thereof. Anyway, a butane barbeque lighter works just fine. I like using the 16.4 ounce propane bottles as they are easy pack and store.

One bottle averages about an hour of cooking time with both burners set on high.

Keep in mind a quart of water boils in about 4 to 5 minutes (depending on altitude). I recommend storing at least one 16.4 ounce propane bottle per day per 4 persons.

If you have room to spare, rigging a 2½ or five gallon propane tank will take all the guess work out of whether you'll have enough fuel. Regardless of how you configure your propane stove, test it at least once a year. Propane lines can deteriorate, clog, and fail, and the larger bottles provide a false sense of security. In other words, it's easier to run out of gas using a five gallon bottle than storing several new small bottles. Note the "T" adapter on the five gallon bottle pictured above which allows fueling more than one appliance at a time.

Tools

While I always carry a set of tools which allow me to perform many basic emergency vehicle repairs, the minimum for storage at the cabin should include the following:

Battery Jumper Cables
Cutting axe
Hatchet
Knife
Multi-tool
Shovel
Sledge hammer
Splitting axe
Wedge

I consider the cutting axe, hatchet, jumper cables, and shovel mandatory. The sledge hammer, splitting axe, and wedge should be considered if you must split larger logs to the size your wood burning stove can handle. The cutting axe is used for splitting smaller pieces of firewood. The hatchet can be used for both cutting firewood and double as a hammer for minor repairs. I keep several shovels handy and always carry one in each of my vehicles. I may have to retrench runoff away from the cabin during a severe storm or dig my vehicle out of getting stuck in the mud.

Shown above is a 6 gallon water jug, the type I recommend for storage of extra water. I have a half-dozen of these I store at the cabin in the event of an emergency. I can easily load these into the back of the truck in a bug out situation. Note the convenient spout which collapses into the jug itself when not in use preventing damage.

The blue color of the jug is intentional indicating the jug is for water only. Never use a blue jug for gasoline or anything else but water. Never use any jug for any content other than what it is rated for.

Battery Jumper Cables

Out of all of the requests for assistance from travelers in all types of vehicles is for a jump start. I never travel anywhere without a quality set of jumper cables. Even my wife has a decent set in the trunk or her car. I recommend cables at least 15 or 20 feet long, you never know what the circumstances might be for reaching each of the vehicles batteries. A good set of jumper cables can set you back around a hundred bucks, but the first time you need them for yourself you will realize the value of a quality tool.

At each end of the jumper cable are two large spring loaded clips often referred to as "alligator" clips. The clips should be enclosed in heavy rubber insulation with the exception of the point of contacts for the battery terminal. The insulation provides added safety from inadvertently causing a short which can be dangerous. The insulation covering the clips at each end of the cable should be color coded; one clip black for ground and one clip red for positive. In addition each clip should be marked with a "-" for negative and a "+" for positive. When connecting jumper cables the rule is always black to ground and red to positive on both vehicles.

Note: Always refer to the vehicle's operation manual for procedures for jump starting. All procedures in the vehicle operation manual for jump starting must supersede any of my suggestions.

Some vehicles have recommended procedures for jump starting as well as preferred locations to install each clip. My truck for example, has a hard point located next to the battery compartment exclusively for connecting a positive clip. This hard point has a removable cover to prevent unnecessary exposure. The negative clip is easily attached to any of the surrounding vehicle chassis. The clips can also be attached directly to the battery posts. If there is any corrosion, or if the ground clip is attached to a painted part of the vehicle chassis, it may be necessary to move the clip back and forth with a little pressure to enable a clean connection.

Note: never jump start a frozen battery. Jump starting a frozen battery could cause the battery to explode.

I connect the positive clips first followed by the ground clips. I remove the positive clips first followed by the ground clips when finished. Once the cables are connected, attempt to start the vehicle with the failed battery with the other vehicle's engine off. If this is unsuccessful, start the engine on the vehicle providing the jump to increase the amount of charge to the failed battery. I have had instances where leaving the engine on for as long as 15 to 20 minutes was necessary to allow the other vehicle to start. Once the vehicle is started remove the cables.

There are many reasons why a battery goes dead and why a vehicle with a failed battery will not start using jumper cables. The best of circumstances probably is when the battery goes dead because the headlights or other accessories where left on. In this case, the vehicle should start up right away.

The driver of that vehicle should not shut off the engine until the battery is fully charged. The colder the weather the more difficult it is to get a vehicle started, so in addition to turning on the engine of the vehicle providing the jump start, you might also try increasing the engine RPM's. Batteries which have gone dead from age will offer the same challenges. The worst case scenario is when any of the cells inside the battery disintegrates. It is not likely a battery in this condition can be jumped. The battery must be replaced.

Duct Tape

Duct tape deserves its' own section for discussion. Duct tape has an infinite number of uses, for example, I've used duct tape as a temporary repair for broken windows by applying lengths of duct tape on both sides allowing the adhesive sides of the tape to adhere. I used duct tape to effect a temporary repair of my favorite pair of boots (the sole had split), and they lasted through the rest of a week I needed them the most. In the picture below I show one way of temporarily repairing a snapped pole for my outdoor canopy. I placed two lengths of spare conduit alongside the part of the pole which snapped, and applied the tape. This is called a splint, and lasted until I could purchase a replacement pole.

Tip: I recommend folding over the end of the tape on the roll about a quarter inch making it much easier to find and pull the end of the tape the next time you need to use it.

Fire Extinguisher

This should be a required piece of equipment and I highly recommend purchasing a 10lb ABC unit. The ABC designation means the fire extinguisher is effective for electrical, grease, flammable liquids, and paper and wood fueled fire. Don't waste your money on the cheap plastic kitchen models and prepare for a price tag of around $100.00. Remember, this piece of equipment can be a life saver inside and outside your cabin. A fire extinguisher also does "double duty" since you can take it with you. I recommend purchasing at least two units, each should be placed in an easy to access area such as close to the wood burning stove and in the kitchen.

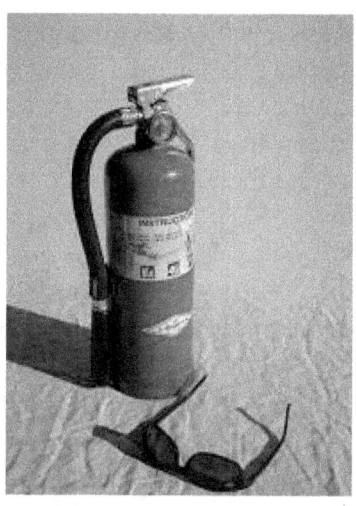

Follow the instructions printed on the outside of the fire extinguisher. The extinguisher contains a dry chemical combined with a compressed propellant. I have (fortunately) only had to use mine a couple times. One time worth noting was when I happened upon a driver who had crashed head on into a large tree. I checked on the driver and thankfully, it was a low speed impact and he was okay. Meanwhile the engine compartment had caught fire and was beginning to spread to a large pine tree.

This was in a dangerous location, in dry forested area, relatively well populated. I decided not to attempt to put the fire out, but instead I hit the spots on the tree at the base of the flame which were igniting with short bursts of the dry chemical. I was able to keep the fire contained to the car for about 10 minutes. And that was perfect timing as the fire department arrived just as I had emptied my extinguisher.

Smaller extinguishers, such as this 10 pound model, come equipped with mounting hardware. If you can't use the mounting hardware for you vehicle, make sure you store it so the pressure gauge cannot be sheared off. And, of course, you don't want the handle mechanism to accidentally deploy.

Note: have your fire extinguishers inspected and refilled if necessary ever five years by a professional. Such inspections are required by law in all commercial establishments but may vary depending upon the jurisdiction..

Flashlight

Another important investment is your flashlights. Odds are you will need a flashlight to light the lantern in case of a power failure.

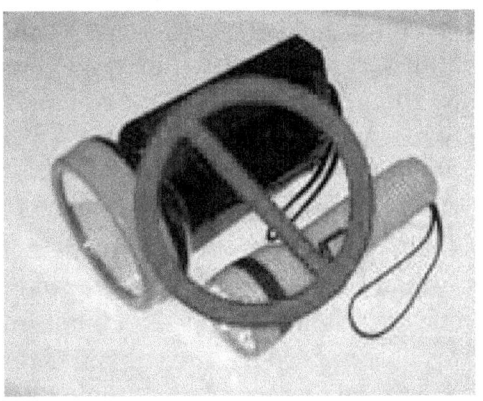

I've tried many different types of flashlights and prefer the models shown below made by MagLite. They are made of aluminum, are extremely durable, and generate more than adequate lighting. Don't bother with cheap plastic flashlights, like the kind sold as a promotion along with batteries. They won't last out the night you need it the most.

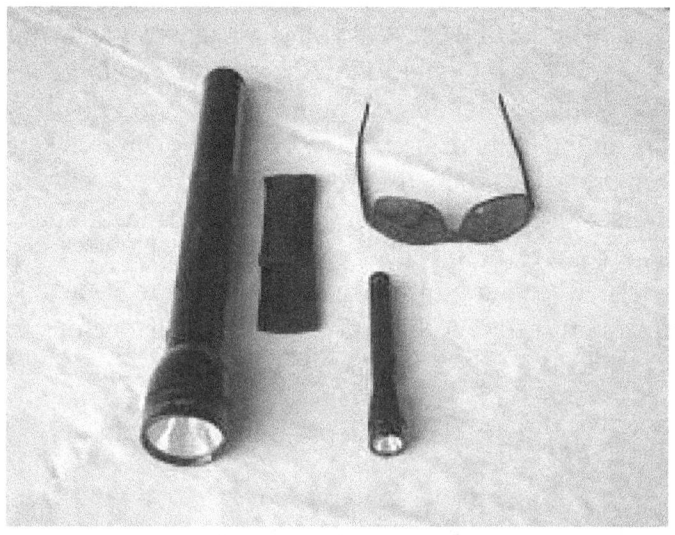

The sunglasses have been placed next to the flashlights to give you some perspective as to size. The larger flashlight is a four cell "D" size, while the smaller is a two cell "AA" size. Both are MagLites and are preferred by law enforcement officers in the field whom I have actually stopped on several occasions and asked for their specific opinion on this subject. The first aid kit is a perfect place to store extra bulbs for each flashlight too. The smaller MagLite comes with a sheath which can be worn on your belt.

I recommend flashlights which use at least two batteries because they last longer in terms of number of hours of light. If you plan to store your flashlights for more than a month with no plan to use them, remove the batteries to prevent leakage and permanent damage.

Knives

Another excellent investment you can make in a hand tool is a knife. Unlike the multi-tool, there are hundreds of quality products to choose from. I prefer a larger fixed blade hunting knife made in U.S.A by Buck Knife. It suits my requirements as an all-purpose tool. I can cut cord, clean fish, and in an emergency even open canned food (although not recommended, you're supposed to have a can opener!). Like your multi-tool, keep your knife clean, sharp, and rust free. A dull knife is far more dangerous than a sharp one.

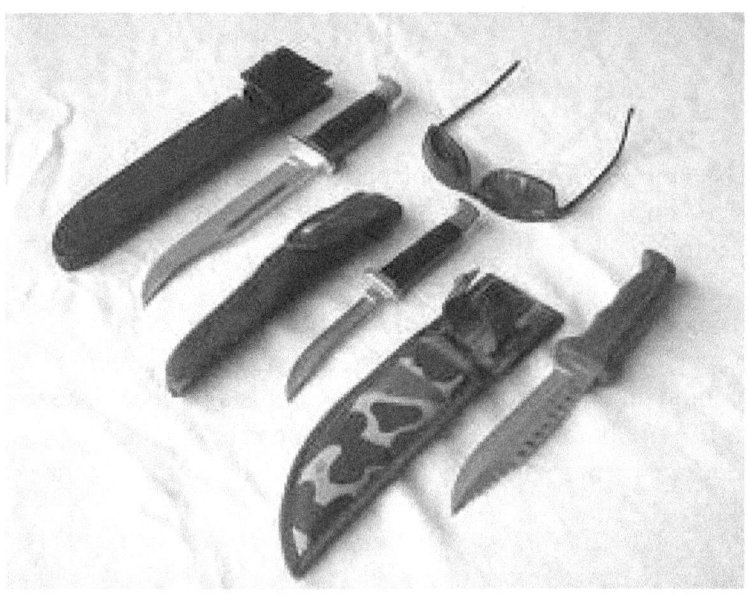

Multi-Tool

By far, the best investment I have ever made in a hand tool is the multi-tool. Don't buy a knock-off, I recommend the one made in U.S.A. by Leatherman, a company which specializes in manufacturing multi-tools. You'll pay $70.00 or $80.00, but it's worth every buck. I wear mine all of the time. Keep your multi-tool clean, sharp, rust free, and it will last a life time.

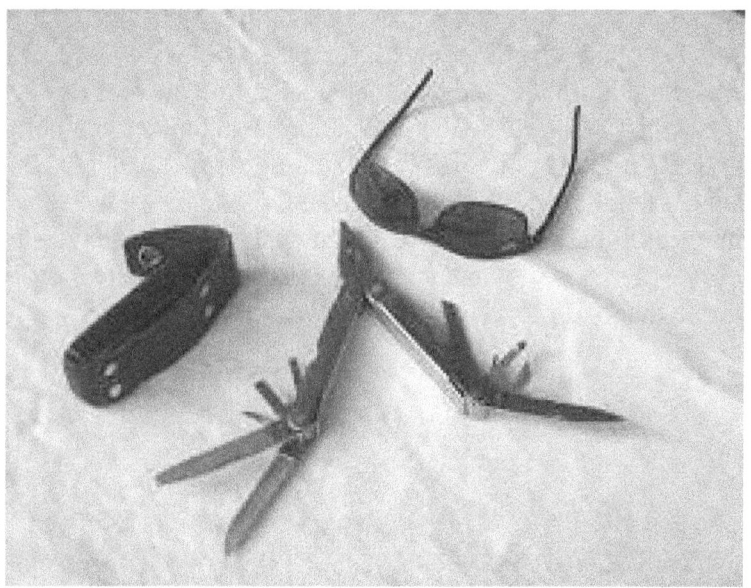

Storage Containers

Rectangular shaped tubs which stack (like those shown below) are ideal for storage of provisions at home and loading into the back of a pickup truck, SUV, or the trunk of a sedan in a bug out situation. The concept here is to be able to load the containers quickly without spending time having to tie them down.

All containers intended for storing provisions (food, toiletries, and other household items should have an effective method of securing the lids to keep the animals out. I have had raccoons actually lift unsecured lids from storage containers and losing a couple months worth of beef jerky, nuts, crackers, just to name a few.

I pack soft bulky items such as sleeping bags, pads, blankets, and pillows into larger heavy canvas duffle bags. Duffle bags are easy to store and in a bug out situation should be the last items to pack, usually on top of the storage containers. Since the duffle bags will be considerably lighter, they will have to be tied down. I don't like cargo nets because they often tangle and take too much time to deploy. Tying off even six or eight duffle bags using a length of rope shouldn't take more than a few minutes if you have to leave in a hurry. Once you are out of the "danger zone", you can take the necessary time to secure the load properly.

Smaller versions of a cabinet or tub showed here work well for packing in trunks or the back of SUV's. Any set of containers which stack are much easier to load, unload, and store. If you use containers with lids, make sure they attach securely, otherwise you'll have to tie them down with bungee cords or cordage.

First Aid Kit

Build your own first aid kit. Buy a heavy gauge plastic fishing tackle box, the kind where two or three shelves unfold as you open it. Most of the items you need you probably already have around the cabin. Building your own first aid kit is much less expensive and the end result is far superior to the expensive store-bought kits. Also, a first aid kit doesn't always have to be synonymous with life threatening emergencies. Include such items as a sewing kit (the kind you get when staying at a hotel, for example), extra shoe laces, and safety pins. And it's a great place to store extra mantels for your propane lantern.

I have included a list of items I carry in my first aid kit later in this guide. I especially like those sample packets for antacids, sun screen, aspirin and so forth. They fit nicely into a tackle box, and you don't have to buy a whole bottle of whatever you have sample packs for. Your first aid kit can double for both camping trips and emergency preparedness around home, so be sure to inspect your kit regularly for expired medications and re-supply if necessary. Whatever space you have left over in your tackle box/first aid kit should be filled with as much extra sterile gauze and elastic bandage in roll form as possible.

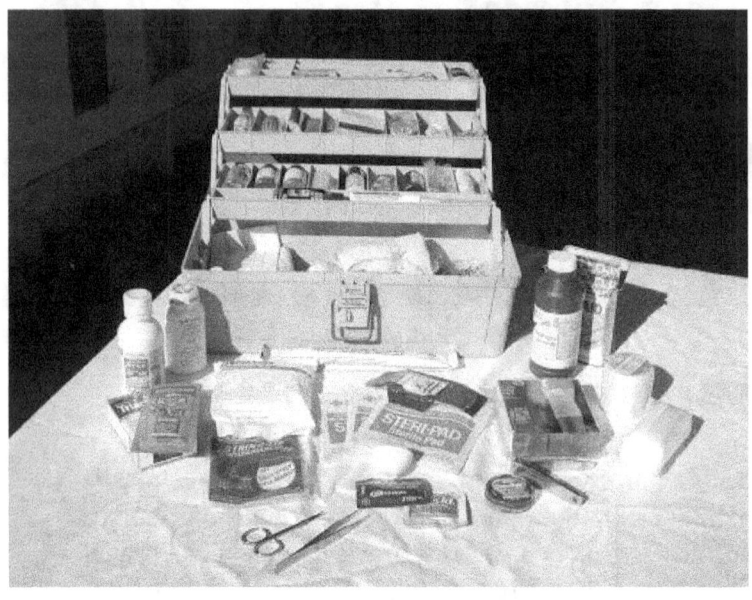

In my opinion, sterile gauze and elastic bandage are likely the two most important materials you'll need in an emergency.

I also add items I wouldn't classify as first aid, but since the tackle box is a convenient place for storage I include the following items as well: toothbrushes, toothpaste, floss, shampoo, comb, insect repellent, whistle, matches, eyeglass repair kit, vinyl repair kit, and a small oil stone for sharpening knives.

Note: I store my first aid kit in my vehicle. In this way I can assure I have it with me wherever I go. Of course I have another at home in case my wife needs it while I am away.

Summary, Equipment

In staying with the theme of keeping cabin living simple, safe, and comfortable, I have detailed the minimal tool and equipment requirements necessary to ensure comfort and safety. However, I would like to offer a few more observations.

Whether the topic is camping, cooking, fishing, or survival, gadgets can end up as your worst enemy. Gadgets demonstrated and sold on TV and over the Internet are always shown to work fantastically. Among my favorites include the camping toaster (I have witnessed someone who tried one of these and the only result was burnt toast), those knives which can cut bolts but then slice tomatoes deli thin (the tang snaps in half after the first use), telescoping fishing rods which last a day if you're lucky, and my favorite, the pocket saw. A piece of steel cable (the diameter of perhaps a bicycle brake cable) with sharp burrs attached at each end to steel key rings. The amount of force necessary to use this tool is far greater than the design will tolerate. The cable will snap from one end or the other before you can finish cutting a small log. Beware of gadgets!

Chapter 7 Enjoying Rural Living

Our cabin is situated above a creek which is dry except during the rainy season. In springtime, when the weather is warm and the creek is flowing, it is a popular area for families to congregate and picnic. The kids have fun running and playing in the water, if not to keep cool. The area was a classic setting with green grass, wild flowers of all colors in full bloom, and lots of large Oak trees for shade. Trouble was, and I wasn't about to crash anyone's picnic, all of the cabins in those mountains had septic systems. Every time there was significant rain, most of those systems would overflow. And that meant overflow into the creek. I could tell because of the distinct odor emanating from the water flowing down the creek. And where do you suppose the kids were playing most of the time! I don't know to this day if anybody ever got sick, but I never allowed any of my guests near that water.

Get to Know the Flora

The moral to my story above is to research trees, bushes, and groundcover indigenous to the area you reside. Shown below is what Poison Oak typically looks like during spring and early summer. There's an old saying: *"leaves of three, let them be"*. Poison Oaks' signature three leaf clumps are easily identifiable but there are many imitators. My general rule is "if you don't know what it is, leave it alone", and this applies to animals as well.

I am using Poison Oak as a specific example because I've had numerous personal experiences with it, and I've done a fair amount of research on the subject. Although the pictures shown here are colorful, Poison Oak can turn dry brown during the winter and can still pack a punch. Deer have been known to graze on Poison Oak when in this condition. Native American Indians would feed the smaller children the chutes of the plant to induce immunization.

Beware, this plant can appear as ground cover, grow as a shrubs many feet in height, and also thrives well by growing as a vine throughout other trees and bushes.

Although I know of no cure for Poison Oak, I have known of folks who swear by a product called Tecnu which is supposedly very effective (for Poison Ivy and Sumac as well) when used to wash affected areas. The next best option if you come in contact is to wash immediately, apply calamine lotion, and do your best not to scratch. The good news is, according to physicians I have interviewed on the subject, Poison Oak is not contagious.

However, I would be careful about coming into contact with your dog if you suspect he's been rolling around in the brush. And, although rare, people who are exceptionally allergic to Poison Oak may develop difficulty breathing if the toxin enters their respiratory tract. They should seek immediate emergency medical attention. Shown here is Poison Oak as it appears in towards the end of the summer season and into early Fall:

Common symptoms from exposure to Poison Oak include a rash that can look intimidating, similar to clusters of mosquito bites. Typically, the rash will begin appearing anywhere from an hour to perhaps a day after contact. Beyond the initial outbreak, the rash may appear to "spread". Actually, the toxin doesn't spread; rather it just takes more time for certain areas of the skin to react depending on the length of contact and level of skin sensitivity.

I've briefly covered the consequences of coming into contact with some of the less desirable plants. I would like to take a moment and review a few more issues that fall into this category. Never, ever let anyone near any type of mushroom. Many mushrooms are poisonous, and most poisonous mushrooms result in death within a short period of time regardless of one's age, gender, or level of health. I instruct all of my guests about the dire consequences of so much as touching a poisonous mushroom. I remind the kids never to kick mushrooms as the debris can result in contact.

Unless you are an experienced botanist, or have been formally trained about edible plants in the wild, I suggest never coming into direct contact with anything in the wild. Berries growing on plants or shrubs are often pretty, easy to pick, and look like they may taste darn good. But, eating just a few may be enough to send a healthy adult to the emergency room.

Rather than scold kids about approaching potentially harmful plants, educate them (and in the process you'll learn something too) about the hazards of touching or ingesting plants and wild fruits without knowing what they are. And be sure to approach a Park Ranger or Docent to ask any questions you may have about the plants which share the environment with you.

Wildflowers and a Big Bite of Humble Pie

On one of my walks into the park I noticed a couple of young ladies who had made beautiful bouquets out of wild flowers nestled in a base of bright red and green leaves from some vine type plant. (Uh, you're not supposed to pick the wild flowers in the park, but that's not my jurisdiction).

I stopped them to compliment them on their creations. "Oh, by the way, do you have any idea what you are holding?" I asked. After acknowledging they had no idea, I informed them they had made the bases of their bouquets out of; you guessed it, Poison Oak! I'm not sure they believed me as they walked away without saying anything. I surmise they found out later though.

On another occasion, I noticed an elderly couple looking very closely at some wild flowers at the end of my driveway. Out of concern for their safety, I casually approached them and advised them to be careful because of the Poison Oak nearby. The elderly gentleman looked up at me and exclaimed "Young man, I am a Professor Emeritus at UCLA Department of Ecology and Evolutional Biology, and I should think I would know what I am doing by now!" I sincerely apologized and proceeded to take my large foot out of my even larger mouth.

Get to Know the Fauna

Take the time to research and educate your guests, including adults, about any poisonous snakes, spiders, and scorpions with which you share your environment.

Snakes come out of hibernation in springtime and when you should also be most vigilant. Be careful when moving rocks out of the way. I have turned up rocks on numerous occasions and found scorpions clinging underneath. Instruct the kids never to put their hands in holes, brush, or anywhere they are not able to see in advance.

I have already mentioned the potential dangers coyotes, big cats such as the mountain lion and bobcat, owls, and hawks present to your pets and small children. However, a couple of examples of harmless critters are worth mentioning. Crows can be pretty obnoxious when they get going with their calling in the early morning. Crows are federally protected migratory birds and fines are severe for harassing or harming them. Rabbits can devastate a garden literally overnight. Take preventative measures such as erecting chicken wire around and above your garden. Be sure to bury it deep enough to prevent rabbits from digging under the fence. Raccoons, if left by their own devises, will enter your cabin through an open screen or window without the slightest bit of fear. You can scare them away a few times, but soon after they lose all fear of you. Keep screens and windows closed and feed your pets inside the cabin.

Be Prepared for Insects

I really only dislike two basic elements of nature which can ruin my day: wind and insects. Wind is simply miserable. If it's going to be too windy, I'll cancel the day's outdoor agenda and catch up on chores without hesitation. Insects are virtually unpredictable. I recommend, and am never without insect repellant and mosquito netting.

Products containing DEET are generally preferred for repelling mosquitoes, ticks, and many types of flies. Insect repellant should only be necessary for use during early morning and the evening when most insects tend to make their presence known. The screens on your doors and windows should protect you at night assuming you keep them shut at all times. Other types of insect repellent containing fragrances actually attract bugs.

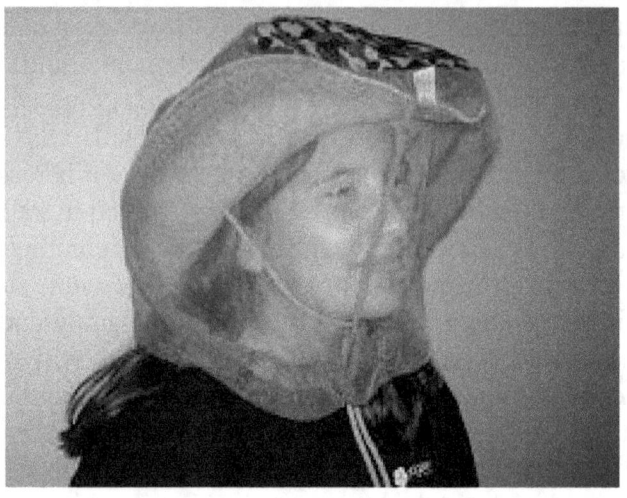

Mosquito netting, or better yet a head net, can be used to place over your head during the day. Secure it by wearing a wide brimmed hat. That'll keep you from performing the Australian Salute every five seconds by keeping biting bugs away from your face, particularly your eyes and ears But, don't forget to lift the head net before taking a drink!

Another pest I am acutely aware of is Yellow Jackets. Yellow Jackets are carnivorous, in other words they go after anything made of meat or meat by-products and that includes you. The stronger the odor, for example an open can of tuna fish, the larger the swarm.

Eating hot dogs outside on the picnic table can be challenging when one is swarmed by these aggressive pests. And getting bit by one is excruciatingly painful. They seem to be worse at different times of the year, so I just plan on having to deal with them. You can purchase traps specifically for Yellow Jackets, but if you can't find them or you are otherwise without the traps, a neat trick is to make your own trap.

Take an empty plastic one gallon water container and cut a few "doors" on opposite sides about 3 or 4 inches from the bottom. Fill the container with a combination of water and a heavy dose of dish soap, ammonia, or bleach about half way to the "doors". Dangle a piece of beef jerky (or sandwich meat) on a string about 3 or 4 inches from the opening at the top of the container. The Yellow Jackets will be attracted to the bait, enter the doors, and ultimately become overwhelmed by the liquid. Place your traps out at the perimeter of your patio because you don't want to get near them for quite awhile.

I have since found online and field tested an extremely effective trap for Yellow Jackets. The trap is a bit expensive, about $15.00 for what amounts to a plastic enclosure with a top and bottom which unscrew allowing for inserting of the bait and emptying it for re-use. But, it's worth every penny. The key to this particular trap is the chemical attractant. Before attempting to use any type of trap, read all of the instructions very carefully. Misuse or making one mistake, could result in a lot of discomfort.

I am going to improve on the instructions a bit based on my experience. Start by using latex gloves on both hands when handling the attractant. The attractant is a liquid which comes in a small tube about the size of a stick of gum. Use scissors to very carefully snip the narrow end of the tube to apply the liquid to the cotton ball. The cotton ball is then mounted inside the trap. Once you break the tube of attractant, I recommend acting quickly. I also recommend having two adults deploy the trap; one to break the tube and apply the liquid to the cotton ball while the other secures the cotton ball (now bait) into the trap and places the trap at the perimeter of the patio.

Meanwhile, the first adult disposes of both the piece of tube snipped off by scissors and the rest of the tube at the oppose ends of the patio from where the trap is placed.

The first time I used this trap I had no idea how effective the attractant is. Within less than a minute the area where the pieces of tube laid on the ground were swarmed with Yellow Jackets. I had to use a shovel to move the pieces of tube to the other end of our front yard. Meanwhile, the trap had already begun to fill up with Yellow Jackets. I learned not to deploy these traps in the area you are trying to rid the pests, but assemble the trap at the location you plan to place it.

Thirty to forty feet from your picnic table should work fine, and you should need only one. This type of trap remains effective for up to two weeks or when it is completely full. If you get any attractant on clothing, immediately change out of the clothing. You may have to discard the clothing. Wash any parts of skin where the attractant has come in contact. You may have to use rubbing alcohol or even acetone (nail polish remover) to neutralize the effect of the attractant.

Vermin

I have always been fortunate to have had rodent problems only as a result of living at the far reaches of the suburbs or rural areas. Most rat and mouse problems are resolved by the owls and coyotes living in the nearby foothills. But every now and then I get an unwanted tenant under the flooring or in the attic. There are several options available to remedy this situation. An exterminator is going to cost you some serious scratch. Laying out poison means the rat or mouse will likely meet its maker while inside a wall meaning you will have to tolerate a rather unpleasant odor for a good while. And, you don't want to risk inadvertently poisoning the neighbor's cat or any of the wild critters which also helps maintain the rodent population. And, those disposable traps where you don't actually see the animal are pretty expensive.

So what do I recommend? Well, you're not going to like it but I recommend the good old fashioned mouse and rat traps. The traps I'm talking about are spring loaded with a bait pedal and a retaining arm. They are inexpensive, no poison, nothing decaying inside your walls. The smaller traps meant for mice are easy to set; simply bait the pedal, grasp the trap with your thumb and index finger on each side of the trap while setting the retaining arm to the bait pedal. Place the trap where mice have been frequenting. Make sure the trap is out of reach of children and pets.

Important note: Rodent droppings can carry an extremely dangerous virus called Hantavirus. If the infestation includes droppings, seek professional help for assistance with clean up before setting any traps.

The larger version of the mouse trap I describe above used for rats is baited and set the same way. I wear a heavy glove when handling a rat trap. The spring loaded bar is powerful enough to break a finger, so you must pay attention. I have seen rats as big as some Chihuahuas, so care must be used when selecting a spot to place the trap.

The bait that works best for me is peanut butter. My last experience getting rid of a rat in my shed took only about an hour! Earlier in the day I had noticed one of my sleeping pads for camping had been chewed though. I set a trap and came back in an hour and my problem was solved! I simply picked up the trap (with the dead rat) and dropped it in the trash can. Cheap, easy, and no mess.

Note: sensitize a mouse or rat trap by slightly crimping the cutout on the bait pedal where the spring loaded bar is set. The critter could actually steal the bait without setting off the trap unless it has been sensitized. But, be careful!

This critter paid a visit to our bath tub. I'm glad I wasn't the first to use the shower after he showed up!

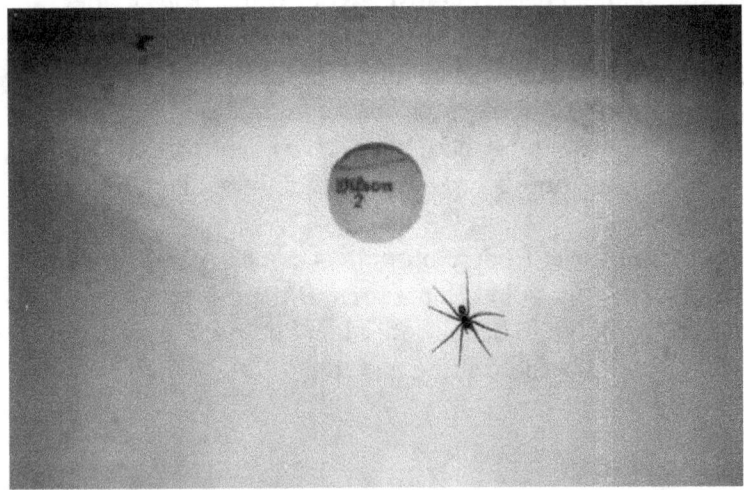

Recreation

Our cabin is located close to an obscure back entrance to tens of thousands of acres of land under the jurisdiction of the Federal Conservancy. Such land is protected from all development, defacing of any structure natural or otherwise, removal of plants, trees, and all other objects, and is patrolled by law enforcement personal to impose these rules. There are many hundreds of miles of hiking and biking trails offering exquisite views in all directions. I have spent many an evening walking into the park if not just for the much needed exercise. My kids spent much of their free time exploring the bike paths and upon arriving home often had stories to tell me about the creatures they saw, potential swimming holes, and caves they had yet to take a peek inside.

Our cabin had a rather long "driveway" almost adjacent to the paved highway and ran almost an eighth of a mile. Our driveway was mistaken for the road on many occasions whereby I would wake up in the middle of the night with headlights shinning in the front window. It never took the driver more than a minute or two to realize his mistake and simply turn around and drive off.

The driveway is mostly straight with a slight slope uphill to the cabin. The "front yard" is a flat area more than enough room for an impromptu half-court basketball court, regulation horse shoe pits, and outside dining and barbeque. In rear of the cabin was an unusual structure we dubbed the "platform". The platform consisted of three large beams, each perhaps 6 by 8 and about 15 feet long. The beams were bolted together forming a triangle shaped frame over which dozens of planks were nailed down.

Each corner of the platform was anchored to a large boulder straddling the creek on the back side of the cabin. Before the fire, the plants and shrubs offered shade if you wanted it, but there was plenty of room for sunbathing. My kids would go "camping" on the platform on warm summer weekends. This picture taken from the back bedroom shows the large wooden board used for the walkway to the platform:

The freedom my kids enjoyed and the activities available to us along with the privacy are admired by all who visit, and are treasured always by us fortunate to live full time in this wonderful setting. But, there are always surprises that come with the territory!

Just Another Lazy Day Pitching Some Shoes

Another warm sunny Sunday afternoon, what could be better than fresh squeezed cold lemonade while tossing horse shoes? My brother had dropped by to visit for the day so naturally we engaged in a little sibling rivalry. My wife was out so it was just the two of us enjoying a quiet peaceful afternoon when all of a sudden we heard a crashing in the brush on the other side of the cabin. The disturbance was loud enough that we weren't about to sprint to the scene, rather we gingerly made our way as quietly as possible to a corner at the rear of the cabin. To our amazement, we had actually caught a bobcat totally by surprise with a large squirrel confidently secured in his jaws. He turned to look at us and as we backed off just as carefully as we approached, he bolted in the opposite direction presumably to have his lunch. I'll never forget the look on my brother's face as we turned to look at each other the first moment we saw the cat! The most amazing part was that we were able to get within about 15 feet of him from behind without him noticing.

It turns out this bobcat lived behind our cabin for a number of years. Every so often he would walk by the side of the cabin where I had a nice view of the hillside while I was taking a shower. He would pass within just a few feet of me.

The Mystery Lady, Walk Right In

You never know who might drop in! One of the many benefits of our cabin location is that we never worried about locking the doors or even leaving the doors and windows open during the day so long as the screens were shut to keep the bugs out. I didn't have to carry my keys and wallet every time I wanted to take a walk and I didn't have to worry about locking myself out of the cabin. Other than friends and family, we rarely saw visitors, except Buster, the neighbor's Labrador retriever. Buster was one of those dogs you only meet once in a lifetime. He had a real personality and I believe he could actually understand much of our conversation. Buster even possessed manners which made many a human being act like a slob. Buster would drop by most mornings to visit me. He knew I worked out of our cabin and that I was usually alone. He always announced his arrival by gently pawing the front screen door. I always had a dog treat for him but he would still stay awhile even after finishing the treat before going about his day.

However, one quiet morning as I was working away at debugging some software applications, a car pulled up followed by the slamming of the car door and before I could get out of my chair I could hear the front screen door open. A young woman came rushing into the living room calling out someone's name then stopped dead in her tracks as soon as she saw me. We were both startled but after a few seconds she realized she had entered the wrong cabin. She apologized and I replied with my own apology because I was unable to direct her to the person she was looking for. After that experience, I kept the screen door locked from then on!

Tourists, Lost But Happy

Every now and then a lost tourist would show up at our door asking for directions or perhaps some water. One sunny Sunday afternoon we were throwing the football around when a couple of young Japanese men drove up in a rather expensive sports car. They produced a map which was way out of our area and pointed to their destination. They were obviously totally lost and could speak only broken English. They were looking for a place to rent horses for the afternoon. I tried to explain that the locals in my area didn't rent out their horses. I asked for them to wait while I dug out a much larger map and pointed to a place which did rent horses. I showed them where we were and gave them directions as best I could by tracing a route on the map with a pencil. The gentlemen were very happy as I gave them my map. They gave me a 5000 Yen note in return (approximate value is about $50.00). Not bad for a map I got for free!

Beginning of the End

Working from home full time for the past eight years allowed me to spend more time exploring the park and the rest of our rural area. I also got to know many of the neighbors who eventually knew I was a full time resident. Many of them commuted long distances or were simply often away on travel. Many of these folks were movie producers, directors, and other well known celebrities in the business who settled in this rural area because it offered sanctuary from those who would otherwise leave them no room for privacy.

Because I ignored their status and respected their privacy, I became the unofficial Neighborhood Watch Captain whether I wanted it or not, but the "job" didn't entail much, mostly just gathering folks exact addresses and phones numbers in the event of an emergency.

My little business which flourished for almost eight years was going down the tubes by leaps and bounds. Radical changes in technology, and the fact that I was just a one man operation, prevented me from staying on top. I was in a niche market and had been gaining additional competition for the past several years. As my client base dwindled, I had to face the reality that my present lifestyle had to change soon out of necessity.

I held on as long as I could by taking odd jobs around the neighborhood, often times helping my wife who had built up quite a little business of her own over the years. In addition to her job at The Village, she took care of various neighbors homes by watering gardens and tending to their pets while they were away. One of my assignments was to take care of one of our neighbor's horses. There were three of them in a single corral on the same property as the home. My job was to feed and water the horses twice a day and, uh-hum, clean the corral itself. Shoveling horse manure because I needed the extra cash was probably the lowest point in my life, but I proved to myself I could do anything if and when necessary for survival. It was a humbling yet very much a learning experience.

Horses, More than I Ever Wanted to Know

On one afternoon I had arrived at the corral to take care of the usual duties. The gate had a latch secured with a pad lock for which I had a key. As I pushed the wheelbarrow in position, I unlocked the padlock and partially disengaged the latch. At this moment I realized I had forgotten to grab the shovel which was a few feet behind me. In the less than five seconds my back was turned, the old mare used her nose to push the latch completely open and all three horses rushed out the open gate. You know that heart sunk feeling when something goes really wrong? Multiply that times a thousand and that's how I felt as I had no idea what to do.

Fortunately, I didn't have to wait long before help was already in progress. One of the neighbor ladies saw the horses bolting down the old canyon road towards the state highway at the Village. She phoned another neighbor a few miles down the road and the horses were successfully rounded up and herded back. I'm not sure what, if anything, I learned from this. All I know is that I made a huge mistake by not paying close attention. Of course I told the owner, he just laughed it off and actually apologized to me for not mentioning his horses were known escape artists. He then handed me a couple of *real* Havana cigars for my "trouble"!

A Sick Horse

Not too long after the Great Escape, I got frantic knocks on my front door about six in the morning. I opened the door to find a lady I didn't recognize anxiously describing the horse up the street that was lying on its side and wouldn't get up. I just thought "here we go again". I told her I was responsible for taking care of those horses and assured her I would take care of the situation. By the time I arrived at the corral, there were at least a half dozen of the neighbor ladies attending to the old mare. I was grateful as they were all experienced horse owners and knew what to do. They had managed to get the mare on her feet and walking around the corral. The problem seemed to be solved and everyone went about their day. When I checked back a little later, the mare was on her side again. I called a veterinarian whose number I was given by one of the ladies earlier that morning. The earliest he could arrive wouldn't be until evening. Meanwhile, I would spend the remainder of the day trying to keep the mare up on her legs.

The veterinarian finally arrived at dusk. He checked the mare over and performed some other tasks involving a garden hose that I would rather not go into detail. After a couple of hours he informed me that it was time to put the mare down. I had no way of getting hold of the owner, and by this time the same crew of ladies from earlier that morning had shown up to check on the mare. There was no other decision I could make, and ironically, this would not be the first time I had to make the decision to put down a horse. I thanked the veterinarian and did my best to console the ladies who had stayed with me throughout this ordeal. They were all visibly upset, but once again, I was the one who was going to have to explain what happened to the owner.

If it wasn't for his wife's presence during my explanation of what happened, I think he would have been much more light-hearted about the whole event. Once again, he apologized for my having to go through all of this, and handed me a couple more cigars! Sometime later he told me he once had to put down a horse with his sidearm, just like in the old west.

Oddly enough, though my passion and preference for means of transportation are really motorcycles, I have gained considerable experience around horses. The only issue I have with horses is straddling a powerful animal weighing perhaps a half-ton with a brain of its' own. On the other hand motorcycles require your complete undivided attention 100% of the time, but at least you are in total command of the machine. I admit I am less than a novice when it comes to horses, and I know I'll take a beating from all of you horse folks. And, you've already read about the horses that got away from me. But I quickly began to take advantage of this recreational activity practically right in my own backyard as many folks were delighted that I would take their horse out for a ride while they were out of town. And I have a few more stories for you to enjoy, all at my expense!

Buddy and Kaiyai

A friend of mine owned a couple of horses he stabled locally. Our itinerary was always to arrive at the stables a couple of hours before sundown so we could let the horses loose in one of the corrals allowing them time to settle down before our ride. After a thorough brushing, cleaning of hoofs, and a bucket of oats, we strapped on the bare back pads and hackamores and headed out to open country.

We rarely rode during the day in the summer because of the heat, and even then we were careful not to run the horses as some nights never dropped below eighty degrees. Besides, night riding offered more of a challenge and we enjoyed having the trails to ourselves. Our destination was usually a country western bar a couple of hours ride from the stable on the opposite side of the canyon. But there were a few perils to traverse along the way, not to mention the way back.

Cactus Ally

Of all the obstacles I can think of, whether hiking, biking, or on horseback, negotiating a narrow path with Prickly Pear Cactus as thick as swamp grass on either side made me tense up so much even the horse could tell. One accidental pull of the reins, or sudden movement on my part, and I was going end up bed side in a hospital room for who knows how many hours of excruciating pain having all the cactus needles removed. Fortunately, this is a short story, this nightmare never became reality.

Fending off the Dogs

My first time out on horseback and coming into contact with all the neighborhood dogs nipping at the horses legs was enough to make it my last time out. My friend showed me an awesome and very effective way to stave off the canines. The dog packs usually approached stealthily from behind us. We knew better and would let them get within twenty yards or so then we would each pull hard on the rein to split in opposite directions coming around 180 degrees and charge the dog pack head on.

Kaiyai was older than Buddy by several years, but Kaiyai was a quarter horse so I was always on top of the dog pack first. I became accustomed to this part of the adventure and actually enjoyed watching the dogs run off with tails between legs!

The Cliff and Tunnel

My friend rode Buddy most of the time while I rode Kaiyai, an older horse with a little less "spirit" than Buddy which suited me fine. The horses weren't ridden as much as they should have been even though there were a couple of ladies who took them out on occasion. They were skittish at times, we just had to pay attention to our surroundings and do our best to anticipate any reactions from the horses from unexpected events. The next couple of obstacles, the "cliff" and the tunnel, each presented unique precautionary measures. The cliff was a shear face of shale at about a 45 degree angle with the trail cutting into the side no more than a foot wide. Beginning the descent from the top is about a fifty foot drop on the business side of the rock face. Slow and easy was the name of the game here.

The tunnel was actually a pedestrian and equestrian tunnel under a highway and always had at least an inch of stagnant water thick with algae. The combination of saturated algae on slick concrete made the footing for the horses slippery at best. Add a low ceiling (we had to crouch forward so as not to hit our heads) slowed our pace to a casual walk.

Quinceanera

Finally, we are out in open country on ground which was not hard packed and could actually enjoy the rest of the ride to our destination without having to be on constant DEFCON I alert. On one occasion, a beautiful sunny summer evening, as we rode past the picnic area we were entertained by a Mariachi band and could take in the aroma of a variety of barbequed cuisine. The event taking place was a Quinceanera or celebration of the transition of a girl to a young lady. Just as we were about to ride past the picnic area, two young, and I might add very attractive, young ladies approached us from seemingly out of nowhere. They wanted a ride with us for a few minutes. We looked at each other, then back at the ladies, then quickly decided OKAY! That part of the ride with our newfound friends lasted only about 20 minutes after which they thanked us and we said *adios*.

We usually arrived at the country western bar around 8 or 9 and the partiers were in full swing. The bar actually had hitching posts out back away from the parking lot and streets. Ironically, all of the times we stopped by this bar, we were the only "cowboys" on horseback! After removing the bare back pads we usually spent an hour or two at the bar. After a couple of drinks, it was time to head home.

I don't know if there was any such thing as RUI (Riding Under the Influence), if there was I might have been a candidate by the time we left the bar. But, a few beers never put our safety in jeopardy, and I enjoyed a relaxing ride home under the night skies.

Night riding during a New Moon was best for star gazing. Horses can see better than humans, especially at night, but one basic rule I learned the hard way. The horse is always going to continue through obstructions such as low tree branches so long as he does not have to change his posture. Since you sit higher than his head, it's your responsibility to keep from getting "clothes lined". On the way home one particular night, I could see I was approaching a low hanging branch. As I got to the branch I gently moved it away from my face as I was passing by. All of a sudden, for some unknown reason, Kaiyai reared up and I fell backwards resulting in my tailbone contacting asphalt, a fall of at least five or six feet. Kaiyai took off at a full gallop but was rounded up minutes later by my riding partner. With nothing broken on me accept my pride, I mounted old Kaiyai and made it back without further incident. I had a sore tailbone for several weeks.

Remember the cliff I described a littler earlier? On yet another night ride on our way back from the bar we began the ascent of the cliff. The trail narrows to perhaps a foot wide with the rock face on my right and a shear drop to my left. It was about midway up the cliff when Kaiyai lost his footing for an instant, recovered, but sent me flying into the rock face. I landed shoulder first and it didn't tickle either. But that incident could have ended much worse as I could have been thrown down the drop off and might never have been able to write this story. My shoulder was badly bruised and sore for weeks, but at least nothing broken. Mounting Kaiyai again, we made it back without any additional excitement.

The Flood

You're probably wondering by now how or why I kept my interest in riding after getting banged up a bit. I'm not sure I know either. Perhaps it was a novelty which didn't wear off right away and I believe my fondness for motorcycles had something to do with it. Riding bikes and horses have a couple of things in common, namely a sense of independence and the pure satisfaction of enjoying the outdoors each in its own unique way.

I recall vividly a rare day ride we took after a particularly big rain storm which left the creeks overflowing from runoff. We started off toward our usual destination, the country western bar, but once we got past the tunnel it was clear we were going to have to take a detour. A lady on horseback headed towards us informed us of a dead horse lying in the middle of the trail about a mile away. I didn't think anything of it, but my riding friend informed me that exposing our horses to that scene could result in a potentially dangerous situation. I didn't question him about specifics; I was quite satisfied with what I already knew.

Taking this detour meant riding trails we had not previously traveled. This was exciting for awhile until we arrived at a totally unanticipated obstacle: It had been raining steadily for the past hour and the creek had swollen into a small river. The question became "Do we turn back and cut our ride short, or do we cross?" We actually pondered this scenario for several minutes before deciding "Let's go for it!" We found a sandy spot level with the water and my riding friend went first as I followed almost immediately.

Amazingly, the horses did not hesitate the river crossing. I had reins in one hand and a death grip handful of mane in the other as we forded the river. I don't know how deep the river was, I do know the horses hoofs were not touching the bottom. I never in my life ever expected to ride a horse across a river just like in some of those old western movies! The water was swift and carried us perhaps eighty or a hundred feet downstream where we exited back onto land and continued that day's adventure. Although the ponchos we brought kept us mostly dry, our jeans were soaked from the thigh down; they never had a chance to dry because we had to cross the river on the way back.

The Overnighter

Now that I think if it, another reason for my attraction to riding horses probably came from my passion for the old west where camping in the outdoors was a necessity rather than a weekend outing for fun. So, I offered the brilliant idea to take an overnight ride deep into the foothills. My riding friend agreed and we packed whatever we could roll up in a sleeping bag which would be tied off to the rear of the bare back pad. We borrowed a couple of old saddle bags from the tack room for important provisions like a couple of cans of chili and couple of six packs of beverage. We began our overnight trip at our usual late afternoon time and rode up one of the major river beds into the foothills beyond for several hours.

We found a level sandy spot up out of the river bed to set up camp. The bare back pads were placed on a tree which had fallen in a convenient horizontal position. Rather than tie the horses we hobbled them allowing them to graze and drink knowing they weren't going to wander very far. A small camp fire warmed our chili and gave us light, and after a four hour ride I was ready to sack out.

The following morning we found the horses within a couple hundred feet happily grazing. The wonderful benefit of bare back pads versus saddles is they only take a few minutes to mount. As we were ready to head back I made the decision to ask my riding friend if I could try riding Buddy for awhile. He agreed without giving it a thought. I approached Buddy, mounted him, took in the reins, and Whoa! Buddy reared up instantly and off I flew! Thankfully I landed on soft sand. Needless to say, my ride on Buddy didn't last very long. I have no idea what caused him to rear, but then again, I know I wasn't born to be loved by all.

Saying Goodbye to Kaiyai

My riding pal called me late one evening and asked if I would go with him to the stables. He didn't say much, he only mentioned he had received a call that Kaiyai was on his side and wouldn't stand up. We stopped at the store along the way and bought about $10.00 or $12.00 worth of apples and carrots with stems and arrived at the stables around midnight. We managed to get Kaiyai on his feet and feeding on the apples and carrots. There seemed to be hope this was just a fluke. The next evening we met the veterinarian at the stable and said our final goodbye to a good friend. Now that Kaiyai was gone, my riding friend moved Buddy to a stable just down the street from his home and set Buddy out to pasture. We said goodbye to Buddy just a few months later. I wonder if Buddy and Kaiyai had a conception of some form of relationship where upon the loss of one would result in the loss of the other in a relatively short period of time.

Above is Buddy with rider paying a visit to our cabin. This picture was taken only a few years after the fire, note how beautifully the native plants and shrubs have re-grown to its former glory.

Chapter 8 A Beautiful Gift, Time to Move On

By all means the birth of my daughter on the last day of the year was a blessing, and I could not have been happier and of course, I still am. But it was time to face fact. My business was all but gone and our cabin lifestyle was no place for a brand new baby. The first sound of an orbiting helicopter after bringing my daughter home sealed the deal. My wife and I formulated a plan of transition from our rural lifestyle to one in the suburbs back in civilization. We chose to move close to my wife's family as soon as we could find a new place. Meanwhile, my wife moved in with her sister temporarily and landed a nice (real) job at a retirement community for active seniors. Some months later, my wife found a new place for us and the move was on. Except for one problem; I *refused* to leave my cabin! Oops! Had I gone mad? My wife spent months looking for a new place to live and acquiring furnishings as we were not going to take any of the furniture we had from the cabin. She worked hard at her new job to provide for a new lifestyle while I just sat there in the cabin in total denial.

After taking a verbal beating by several other family members, and without my knowledge or consent, had also contributed to our relocation effort, I relinquished by promising to leave the next day. One truck load of belongings later standing alone in front of my beloved cabin where I spent almost twenty wonderful years of my life, I quietly said goodbye.

In retrospect, I know I experienced some level and form of agoraphobia, one definition of which is fear of leaving one's home. It took many years for me to adjust and I still have dreams of life back at our little cabin. But the timing was right as developers moved in and transformed our canyon from a small rural town setting into an extension of the wealthier enclaves which had already encroached upon previously undeveloped land leveling mountain tops and terracing hillsides as far as the eye could see. A different cross-section of people emerged as well, neighbors no longer knew one another nor did they make any effort to do so. Cabins were leveled and replaced by stucco "ranch" homes. The only highway in and out of our canyon became a parking lot everyday because it wasn't designed to handle the large volume of traffic introduced by massive development.

My daughter will become independent, all too soon of course, and I can take comfort that I will once again thrive in a rural cabin lifestyle. And the next time around it won't take me almost twenty years to learn the ropes!

Appendix A Emergency Preparedness (Bug Out) Equipment and Provisions List

Among my passions is backpacking and camping I've been on hundreds of outings and just like a flight plan, I still prefer to have a list of necessary equipment and provisions I can refer to for both camping and my emergency preparedness plan. I have "borrowed" from my camping list and adapted it to part of an emergency preparedness plan for rural living. Compose one for yourself!

[ ] *"The Essentials of Cabin Living, What You Need to Know"*

[ ] Axe
[ ] Bath tissue

[ ] Binoculars; **Tip:** the better quality the binoculars, the happier you will be viewing features which will be better enhanced both in daytime and nighttime.

[ ] Boots, Shoes

[ ] Buckets; **Tip:** a five gallon bucket is an extremely versatile piece of equipment. They're useful for washing dishes, laundry, or handy for putting out a campfire.

[ ] Can opener
[ ] Cash, a couple of blank checks
[ ] Cell phone, charger
[ ] Chairs
[ ] Cooking utensils, pots, pans

[ ] Coolers
[ ] Cork screw
[ ] Dish soap, sponge
[ ] Duct tape

[ ] Extra vehicle key, store somewhere outside the vehicle, perhaps in a storage container. I definitely do not recommend one of those magnetic hide-a-key gadgets. I've lost every one I've tried.

[ ] Fire extinguisher
[ ] Firewood
[ ] Flashlights, extra batteries

[ ] Games: Board Games, Bocce Balls, Frisbee, Glow Sticks, Horse Shoes, Kite, Playing Cards

[ ] Gloves
[ ] Hats
[ ] Hot dog sticks
[ ] Insect repellant
[ ] Insect traps
[ ] Knife
[ ] Lady Campers – That Time of the Month
[ ] Lantern
[ ] Lighter fluid

[ ] Maps; **Tip:** Use transparent plastic contact sheeting to laminate paper maps. This protects the maps from the elements and they last longer.

[ ] Matches; **Tip:** take wood stick matches and waterproof by submerging the tip of the match in melted candle wax. I have matches I waterproofed some forty years ago, and they still work!

[ ] Mosquito netting
[ ] Multi-Tool

[ ] Pillows, blankets (optional, but consider for traveling)

[ ] Plastic bags (Trash, Freezer Storage Bags, etc)
[ ] Ponchos, Rain Suits
[ ] Prescription medications
[ ] Propane
[ ] Paper plates, cups, napkins
[ ] Portable potty
[ ] Radio, portable AM, 2 way, CB
[ ] Rake
[ ] Reading and sun glasses
[ ] Rope, 50 feet ¼ inch, and 100 feet 3/8 inch
[ ] Scarves
[ ] Shade (collapsible shade or umbrellas)
[ ] Shovel
[ ] Sleeping bags
[ ] Sleeping pads
[ ] Stove
[ ] Sun glasses, strap
[ ] Sun screen
[ ] Tents, poles, stakes, rain flies
[ ] Tool box
[ ] Toothbrushes, toothpaste, floss

[ ] Towline - A 20 foot length of chain with hooks on either end for heavier vehicles, About a 30 foot length of 3/8 inch cable with hooks on either end, and a 15 foot nylon towline rated for 6,000 pounds.

[ ] Water jug (5 to 6 gallons, full)

Appendix B First Aid Kit Checklist

[ ] Alcohol swabs
[ ] Baby powder

[ ] Bandages, recommend 3 inch by ¾ inch, you can always trim them down.

[ ] Cloth surgical tape, 2 inches by 10 yards.
[ ] Cotton swabs
[ ] Elastic bandage, 3 or 4 inches by 10 yards

[ ] Gauze, sterile, twenty 4 inch by 4 inch pads, and a couple rolls of 3 inch by 10 yards.

[ ] Hydrogen Peroxide, 8 ounce bottle

[ ] Antacid
[ ] Antibiotic ointment
[ ] Antiseptic

[ ] Cold and cough medication in both adult and little camper strengths

[ ] Hydrocortisone
[ ] Ipecac syrup*
[ ] Menthol rub

[ ] Candle
[ ] Eye wash cup**
[ ] Lantern mantles
[ ] Hand lotion
[ ] Hand soap
[ ] Nail clippers
[ ] Oral thermometer (non-mercury/non-glass)

[ ] Safety pins
[ ] Sewing, button kit

[ ] Shampoo, conditioner (I save those small containers provided by hotels)

[ ] Shoe and boot laces
[ ] Surgical scissors
[ ] Tweezers, one each small and large size

* Ipecac syrup is used to induce vomiting in certain emergency situations. Only certified medical personnel should be consulted regarding appropriate use of Ipecac syrup.

** The eyewash cup is a small plastic, oval shaped cup which fits over the eye socket. I have used it for removing small debris from underneath the eyelid. Fill with distilled water and placed over the eye, then blink to remove the debris. This simple little gadget can save your whole trip.

Appendix C Knots and Tie Downs

There are three basic knots I use frequently. These knots are easy to learn to tie and will work for any situation requiring the securing of rope or cordage

Taunt Line

The Taunt Line (also known as three "half hitches") may be used to tie down everything from the heaviest loads (for example, appliances), or the guy lines on my camping shower. Just like a load shifts on a moving vehicle, the guy lines on camping equipment also shift as a result of wind, soft ground, or me tripping over them. It only takes a few seconds to tighten them all up. Another added bonus is unlike spaghetti knots, half-hitches are easy to untie allowing the cordage to be reused.

In the picture above, I have strung the rope through a hard point followed by making two loops on the inside of the knot (towards the hard point). Take the end and string it towards the outside of the knot and make the final loop. Tighten the knot and you will now be able to slide the knot up the rope to secure your load.

Square Knot

The Square Knot is another simple knot primarily useful for tying smaller lengths of rope together to make a longer length of rope. Tied correctly, the Square Knot will not slip or untie due to stress from securing even the heaviest of loads. And the Square Knot is easy to untie allowing the cordage to be reused.

Tying a square knot is similar to double tying your shoe laces. Loop the rope end held in your left hand over the rope end held in your right hand. So far, you have tied half the knot. Loop the end of the rope which originated in your left hand over the end of the rope which originated in your right hand. Tighten the knot by pulling each length of rope.

Bowline

Mountaineers and rock climbers depend on this knot with their lives. Unlike the Taunt Line which may need to be tightened periodically due to stress, the Bowline will not slip. The Bowline is used primarily to tie of one end of a rope to a hard point such as a tree while the other end might be secured to tent poles using the Taunt Line as an additional anchor against high wind.

Loop the rope around the hard point you wish to tie off to using the Bowline knot. In the example above I am demonstrating how the Bowline is effective to tie myself off. In this example, I loop a section of rope around my left hand. Keeping the loop rigid, I pull a section of rope though the loop creating another loop. The other end of the rope (painted orange) is strung through the loop which I had just pulled through the first loop.

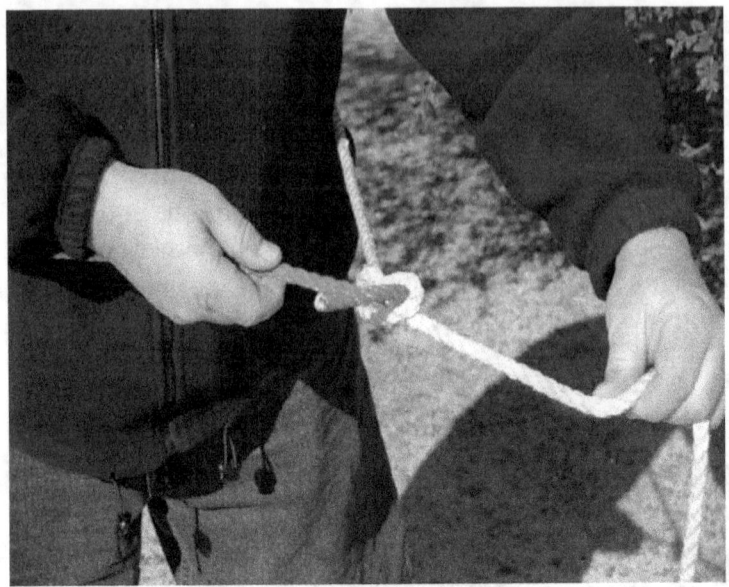

The picture above shows that pulling on the rope away from the Bowline tightens the knot. The Bowline knot will easily accommodate your own weight and potentially even more, assuming the cordage is rated appropriately.

Index